EAST AFRICA FORCE

DESPATCH

31 December 1939

by

Major-General D.P. Dickinson, DSO, OBE, MC

Introduction by
Gerry van Tonder

Edited by
Dr Anne Samson, Great War in Africa Association

GWAA / TSL Publications

The Great War in Africa Association

First published in Great Britain in 2024
By GWAA / TSL Publications, Rickmansworth

ISBN: 978-1-917426-06-0

Cover, maps and illustrations
courtesy of :
Gerry van Tonder

Introduction

THE EAST AFRICAN THEATRE WWII
Gerry van Tonder

At the outbreak of World War Two, the strategic conduct of all the fighting in the African theatres was in the hands of General (later Field Marshal) Archibald Wavell KCB, CMG, MC. There were three main bases for the African campaigns: Cairo, Khartoum and Nairobi.

In anticipation of all-out war in Europe, in June 1939 Britain established the Middle East Command to oversee operations in the Eastern Mediterranean and Middle East theatres. Based in Cairo, General Wavell was appointed as General Officer Commanding, and as the war progressed, his command was extended to include Ethiopia, Eritrea, Libya and Greece.

Thus, with ultimate strategic control emanating from Cairo, Khartoum would provide the British and Commonwealth forces which conquered Eritrea and liberated Northern Ethiopia, while from Nairobi, the East African Force would capture Jubaland and Italian Somaliland, retake British Somaliland, and liberate the rest of Ethiopia, including the capital Addis Ababa.

Fascist Expansionism

As the clouds of war gathered once again over Western Europe, the Italian Fascist empire of East Africa was also flexing its muscle.

Away from her insular existence on the international stage, in 1890 Rome officially laid claim to an African multi-cultural conglomerate of kingdoms, sultanates and chiefdoms delineated by the European empires' scramble for Africa as Eritrea. Then in 1908, Italy established *Somalia Italiana* along the Indian Ocean east of British Somaliland and the Kingdom of Ethiopia, the exonymic Abyssinia. The port city of Mogadishu became the Italian Somaliland colony's capital.

Previously, Italy's designs on incorporating Ethiopia into its growing foothold in East Africa ended in disaster in 1896 when Ethiopian forces defeated the invading Italians at Adwa. The Treaty of Versailles, signalling the end of World War One, further dashed Italy's colonial aspirations on the African continent when, as a consoling afterthought, Britain "gave" Rome a piece of desolate real estate to the east of Kenya, called Jubaland.

The ascendancy to power of Italian fascist Benito Mussolini in October

1922 saw a dramatic surge in the state's national pride, fuelled by the dictator's flamboyant rhetoric. Not unlike Adolf Hitler's Nazi quest for *lebensraum*, Mussolini's foreign policy centred on a doctrine of *spazio vitale*, "living space", under Italy's rule and protection. He had a vision of a latter-day Roman Empire encompassing the whole of the Mediterranean, and northern and eastern Africa from the Atlantic Ocean to the Indian Ocean. Mussolini's prime objective, his "sacred mission", was to take Ethiopia. By the end of 1936, most of Ethiopia had fallen under Italian control.

Over the next four years, the Italians established a "revolutionary" network of first-rate roads, many of them tarmacked. Ironically, this very infrastructure would one day work against the Italians in favour of Allied forces. Of increasing concern to Britain, however, was that by June 1940 a well-equipped Italian army of 300,000 troops had firmly established themselves in the three Italian-controlled territories.

In comparison, Commonwealth forces in East Africa, at the time, were weak in the face of such strengths. In British Somaliland, a battalion of the Camel Corps and a sprinkling of irregulars were responsible for the 500-mile frontier facing Ethiopia. To the south, all that stood in the way of any potential Italian invasion into Kenya and Tanganyika were two King's African Rifles (KAR) brigades of the East Africa Force, commanded by Major-General Douglas Povah Dickinson DSO, OBE, MC (1886–1949). The front stretched for 900 miles.

Finally, and to further expose British East Africa's vulnerability, to the northwest, under Major-General Platt, only three battalions of the British Army and some 4,000 troops of the Sudan Defence Force held Anglo-Egyptian Sudan.

Strengths of the Colonials
Between 1894 and 1911, 3,517 white settlers had arrived in the British East Africa Protectorate, which became known as Kenya in 1920. The vast majority took up farming. Of this number, around 20 percent were Afrikaans-speaking South Africans.

The bulk of the settlers of British nationality would have been said to belong to the upper-middle and "superior" classes at home. At least a third had been to university and a half to a public school, while a minimum of one in five had served in one of the armed forces. About one in ten had previously been to South Africa as soldiers, settlers or civil servants.

More remarkable was the number of parsons' sons. There were at least 41 of them—roughly one in every five officers. Among the others, whose family backgrounds are known, there were 4 sons of civil servants, 12 sons of regular officers, 5 doctors' sons, 5 lawyers' sons, 3 schoolmasters' sons, 9 businessmen's sons, 7 gentlemen's sons, a son of a Colonial Secretary, 2 relatives of a Colonial Under Secretary, and 3 sons of peers.

Thus the colonial administrators, too, came from similar backgrounds. World War One put their class characteristics in stark highlight. Backed by considerable military experience, and buoyed by their senses of patriotism, honour and duty, a large majority, including many Afrikaners, volunteered for active service. The settlers were zealously loyal to the colony. Unstoppable and, along with taking up arms, they entered into general governance wherever it had to do with the conduct of the war. They were the power on the country's War Council and, inter alia, responsible for introducing the first conscription in the British Empire. Serving on many government committees, it is hardly surprising that they also used these positions to consolidate their political standing.

In planning post-World War One developments, they promoted a scheme whereby 1,000 farms were set aside to attract former soldiers to settle in the colony. Among the many reasons for their support was the appreciation that the war had trained many Africans as soldiers in the King's African Rifles (KAR) who, now proficient in arms, might become a problem for white settlers in peacetime.

The official Soldier Settlement Scheme, which was launched both in Kenya and London in 1919, greatly enhanced the already strong military cast of Kenya's settler population. Applicants had to satisfy stringent capital requirements such as possession of £1,000 and a £200 annual income, which tended to restrict settlement to a small wealthy stratum of English society.

Nearly all the non-local participants in the scheme, 550 of a total 685, were officers. They included 9 generals, 61 colonels and lieutenant colonels, 113 majors, 183 captains and 128 lieutenants from the British Army. Another 31 were Royal Navy officers and 25 were Royal Air Force officers. The rest were divided among 41 privates and non-commissioned officers (NCOs), 43 women (some acting as legal "dummies" for husbands) and 51 unknown.

The arrival of these former servicemen bolstered the British element of the settler population. In addition to retired servicemen, retired officers from Crown service were now also encouraged to become settlers. The immediate post-war governor, Sir Edward Northey GCMB, CB, who, in World War One had commanded the Nyasa-Rhodesia Field Force operating against General Paul von Lettow-Vorbeck's indigenous and

German forces in the East African Campaign, had persuaded Lord Alfred Milner, the Colonial Secretary, to approve participation by officials in the scheme.

The Soldier Settlement Scheme of 1919 must rank as one of the most significant events shaping Kenya's white settler community. By the time the scheme was completed in 1921, the white population had risen to 9,651. Naturally, many different personal reasons would have brought members of this social stratum to Kenya, and if, collectively, the settlers exhibited distinguishing characteristics, then it is reasonable to suspect a common cause. Their belief in themselves and in what they were creating was unshakeable.

In 1905, the East African Volunteer Reserve Ordinance (VRO) was proclaimed, giving official sanction to the creation of a white militia, which would be comprised of both mounted and infantry units. However, the Colonists' Association argued that the settlers were too few and dispersed for such a force to be effective.

In 1911, the VRO was revised and, despite previous resistance to a national defence force, allowed volunteers to opt for colony-wide "field" service. Within a year the number of settlers joining had increased to 431. Through the VRO the first military units, comprised of white settlers in what became Kenya, came into being, though there is no record that they were involved in any actions.

The Great War Experience

When war was broke out in August 1914, the East African Protectorate (Kenya) was altogether unprepared, whereas the Germans in their neighbouring colony, German East Africa, had been anticipating the event for some time. Seven months earlier they had posted an officer of outstanding ability, Lieutenant-Colonel Paul von Lettow-Vorbeck, to take command of the Schutztruppe, their indigenous defence force.

It is therefore hardly surprising that unfounded rumours spread throughout the country that Nairobi was in danger of imminent invasion, resulting in much of the white population converging on Nairobi. In *White Man's Country*, author Elspeth Huxley captures the moment:

> On August 4 a volunteer enlistment office was opened in Nairobi House. The first wave of excitement washed hundreds of Settlers through its doors. Some had paused only to seize a rifle and pocketful of ammunition and to saddle up a mule before riding into the capital. Many of the Uasin Gishu Settlers [Afrikaans-speaking farmers] arrived in a body.

The news reached them in the midst of an agricultural meeting at Eldoret [in the White Highlands, 165 miles northwest of Nairobi]. They leapt on to their waiting mules, rode through part of the night to the nearest station at Londiani, boarded a train and arrived some thirty-six hours later—hungry, unshaved, without clothes or money. Some of them had fought against the British fourteen years before [Second Boer War].

The volunteers brought their own rifles, ranging from huge double-barrelled elephant guns to light carbines. Some were provided with ammunition, some were not. Uniforms varied according to each man's taste. His hat might be a khaki helmet, a battered felt with an ostrich feather tucked into one side, or even a cloth cap. His shirt was generally a sort of tunic with huge pockets, and sleeves chopped off at the elbow. He might wear shorts, breeches or slacks; gaiters, puttees or even tennis shoes. A bright handkerchief was often knotted around his neck, a bush knife stuck into his belt. His mount was often a mule and generally a vicious, obstinate and uncontrolled one at that. He was hung about with homemade bandoliers, water-bottles, tins and anything that occurred to him as potentially useful.

Initially, there was a complete lack of any order or discipline and, as the bars in the town were open all night, despite the declaration of martial law, rumours abounded of an imminent invasion by legions of "Squareheads" (foreigners of Germanic origin) and the possibility of an air attack, the enemy having been quite erroneously credited with possessing a large air force.

However, having reported for duty to Nairobi House, which had become the Volunteer Forces' Headquarters, these enthusiastic irregulars initially organised themselves into bands; the Boer settlers forming the "Plateau South Africans".

The well-known settler, Russell Bowker, sporting a snarling leopard's head skin for a cap, rallied his followers into "Bowker's Horse". Other volunteers formed Arnoldi's, Ross' and Wessels' Scouts. It was out of this almost anarchic but enthusiastic diversity that the East African Mounted Rifles (EAMR) came into being. The units were consolidated into a single corps of mounted volunteers comprising six squadrons, each with Maxim gun and signalling sections. By the end of August 1914 the unit comprised over 400 volunteers.

In the very early days of the war, the EAMR served briefly on the border between East Africa Protectorate and German East Africa (later Tanganyika, then independent Tanzania). Given their backgrounds and experience in both British and Boer armies, its members were too valuable to be retained as troopers in a small, mounted corps. It was therefore inevitable that, within a few months, the majority were transferred as officers and NCOs to other units. This allowed very rapid expansion of the King's African Rifles (KAR), in which Africans formed the other ranks. The record of the EAMR is virtually unequalled as regards the proportion of men who received commissions from the ranks.

Post-war Politics and Defence

At the end of World War One, the concept of a settler military body was raised at an EAMR reunion. Arising out of this, the Settlers' Convention of Associations appointed a committee to review the proposal. This body recommended that a defence force be established with the compulsory enlistment of all white males between 16 and 60 years of age.

At this time, the white settlers saw their dream of the East Africa Protectorate developing into a self-governing dominion threatened by a numerically superior Indian population. In simple terms, the white settlers were not prepared to have a largely illiterate Indian population wrest the reins of political and economic power from them. Such was the fervour, that in August 1921 and January 1923 some settlers spoke of taking up arms to force their case.

The threat of a colonial revolution shocked Whitehall, but it would take the return of a Conservative government under Prime Minister Stanley Baldwin in 1924 to turn the settlers' fortunes back to where they were. In November 1926, the Defence Force Bill was eventually published.

In what many construed as a political move, the bill provided for the compulsory enlistment of every white male in the protectorate between the ages of 16 and 60. In 1928, the Kenya Defence Force (KDF) was established. Registration started in July that year, and by October, 4,518 (86 percent) of the 5,229 whites liable to service had registered.

A return of Labour in Britain in June 1929 saw significant cuts to the KDF's budget, resulting in wholly inadequate training of those in the Class I combatant age group. Whilst five-day camps continued to be held at Eldoret, such musters increasingly became an excuse for heavy drinking sessions at the nearby Soy Hotel.

The appointment of anti-settler Governor Sir Joseph Byrne GCMG, KBE, CB, in 1931 brought fresh disquiet within the white community, leading to a polarisation between them and the colonial government. This development was of such concern to Byrne that, in 1934, he sent a secret despatch to the Secretary of State, expressing his grave concern that the KDF "as present constituted is of negligible military value and potentially a source of danger". He recommended,

> That steps should be taken without delay to establish some effective organisation of the White manpower of the Colony. His Majesty's Government should be asked to order the disbandment of the Kenya Defence Force and the establishment of a security force and of a volunteer rifle company in Nairobi and possibly a smaller unit in Mombasa.

In February 1936, Secretary of State Leo Amery fully endorsed Byrne's recommendation, but when this correspondence leaked into the public domain, KDF commander, Brigadier General Arthur Lewin CB, CMG, DSO, resigned in protest at not having been consulted.

There was an explosion of protest from the settler community. Lord Francis Scott and Major Ferdinand Cavendish-Bentinck, the two white unofficial members of the Executive Council, immediately resigned. Lord Scott's missive to Byrne was unbridled: "On what grounds has the Secretary of State come so definitely to this conclusion; a conclusion which, of course, is a big affront to everyone who has been a member of the Kenya Defence Force."

The Kenya Regiment

Byrne was thoroughly stunned by the white community backlash, and he immediately appointed a committee, chaired by Colonel John Alexander Campbell DSO, to "Consider Suggestions for the Reorganisation of the Defence Forces of the Colony". Ten weeks later, the committee published its report, recommending:

> That the Kenya Defence Force be disbanded and replaced by a Volunteer Force up to the strength of a battalion, to be known as "The Kenya Regiment (Territorial Force)" drawn from men between the ages of 18 and 35 and in special cases up to 45, with a Compulsory Force to be called "The Kenya Auxiliary Force" consisting of the balance of able-bodied European British male subjects in the Colony.
>
> We recommend that service in the Kenya Regiment (Territorial Force) should be for a minimum period of four years, and that every member of this Force should put in

twelve days' camp every year, and at least 100 hours of training parade.

The Campbell Report set the proposed Kenya Regiment's primary role in the words "to supply officers, non-commissioned officers, and instructors for the expansion of the Kings African Rifles."

This was Britain's primary East African colonial regiment, founded in 1902, and with battalions in Kenya, Uganda, Tanganyika and Nyasaland. It was officered by men on secondment from the regular British Army, with a quotient of regular British non-commissioned officers (NCOs). The rank and file were drawn from local tribesmen who also provided NCOs up to regimental sergeant major (RSM) level. During the height of World War Two, the KAR had expanded to 44 battalions, heavily officered up to company commander level by white men from the Kenya Regiment (KR).

It was also proposed that a permanent staff of instructors (PSI) should be sought from the Brigade of Guards, and that these be on a minimum basis of one PSI per company, in addition to a serving officer as staff officer or adjutant. Nominally, at least, the KR would have a core of regular British Army officers which, in turn, would make it difficult for the unit to act independently of British government knowledge.

Government accepted the recommendations and the Defence Forces of the Colony were reorganised in 1937. His Majesty gave assent to the Kenya Regiment Ordinance 1937/52, and these forces were established by the Governor in notices in the Gazette of 1 June 1937.

South African-born Acting Lieutenant Colonel Alfred Dunstan-Adams OBE, MC and Bar, TD, was the first commander of the KR (1937), a position he held until 1940 when he became honorary colonel until 1963 when he stood down. Prior to that, he had commanded the KDF's 1st (Nairobi) Battalion.

Qualified as an accountant before World War One, he joined the South African forces in 1914 and saw action in German South West Africa. In 1915 he went to Britain to join the army, specifically the regiment of his grandfather's county: the Devonshire Light Infantry. But he was seconded to the Border Regiment, whose accent he never did get to understand in spite of seeing action with them in Mesopotamia against the Turks and Arabs, and a further three years on the Western Front. He was a battalion commander with the Borders and ended World War One as a brevet lieutenant colonel with two Military Cross awards.

He and his wife Eileen arrived in Kenya in 1924 where, after a few years of unsuccessful farming, he set up an accountancy partnership in Nairobi. In September 1939, Dunstan-Adams re-enlisted, and remained in command of the KR until the Abyssinian Campaign when he became Area Commander, Nanyuki and North.

Recruiting was inaugurated in a letter to the press signed by the governor, calling on young men to join the regiment. The response was immediate and enthusiastic. It confounded the pessimists who had doubted the spirit of the young men of the colony. Out of an estimated number of 2,000 eligible men, over 500 of the type required had enrolled before the end of June.

With the absence of Dunstan-Adams away at King George VI's coronation, Captain Lennox-Browne commanded the regiment during the initial recruiting period. With Lord Stratheden and other officers, he was responsible for interviewing and enlisting the first 500 men.

The battalion was organised with its headquarters and that of No. 1 Company in Nairobi, No. 2 Company in Nakuru and No. 3 Company in Eldoret. In February 1939, a fourth company was authorised.

Training began in August 1938, with all the members having been uniformed and equipped. The first annual camp was held in March 1938 on the slopes of the Ngong Hills, located to the southwest near Nairobi. The general principle adopted for training was that arms-drill, weapons-training, section-leading and minor platoon tactics were carried out during the year, and the annual camp was given over to platoon, company and battalion tactical training with one afternoon for sports.

The KR's second camp in August 1938 was again held at Ngong Hills. It was deemed a success, with 534 soldiers attending. The training had progressed more rapidly than had been hoped for by the most sanguine. This did not mean that the men were fully trained soldiers but it did mean that they had come a long way from being raw recruits. At least 75 percent were capable of instructing in the use of rifle and Bren gun, and more than that number had acted with greater or lesser success as junior leaders in the main tactical exercises and taken part.

However, they still lacked administrative training and had little idea of the ordinary duties of NCOs in an African battalion. However, the majority were holding positions of moderate responsibility, and nearly all could speak Swahili and had had some experience of African labour. Best of all, they were keen and anxious to learn.

War Mobilisation

On August 26, 1939, the commanding officer was ordered to report for duty at Northern Brigade HQ, with instructions to bring the mobilisation posting lists up to date. On the 28th, the first calling-up telegrams were sent to country members and the town members ordered by telephone or orderly to report for duty.

The boys' boarding block at the European Primary School, Nairobi, was put at the regiment's disposal as a mobilisation barracks. As fast as men came in they were mustered into parties and sent off to various battalions of the KAR as junior officers and senior NCOs. By September 3, over 240 officers and men were already with the KAR.

In the middle of September, the battalion moved to the Nairobi Show Grounds (now occupied by No. 1 General Hospital), and on October 6, it moved to Kampala, Uganda.

The Reconnaissance Platoon had returned to Nairobi from Nanyuki and, after re-equipping, was divided into two sections. One section returned to Nanyuki where it was attached to 5KAR and the other went to Garissa where it was attached to 4KAR. Later this platoon was again withdrawn and increased in strength—largely from the regiment—to become the East African Reconnaissance Squadron, popularly known as the "Rekkies". The KR remained in Kampala until the end of the year. At the beginning of January 1940, it moved into camp on the racecourse at Eldoret.

Eldoret was the only town in Kenya that was started by South African Afrikaners who escaped British rule after the Second Boer War. The town was the heart of the Boer community that settled in the area in the early 1900s when Kenya was a British colony.

When the KR basic-training centre was moved from Kampala to Eldoret in January 1940, the men encountered raw conditions. Private John Pitt, a Rhodes scholar and a member of the Colonial Forestry Services, wrote:

> On arrival at Eldoret we found that the depot was the race-course, that the deluxe accommodation was two in a horse box and that we, as later arrivals, had to sleep in an unfinished wooden building intended as a bath house, but still with no floor. Sleeping on the ground was, I suppose, no real hardship in view of what was likely to be in store for us. A further introduction to this was when the rain came and we had, during the night, to dig out the soil on which we were lying to build ramparts to keep out the water!

By this time over 500 members were serving, besides other units, with the KAR, Northern Rhodesia Regiment (NRR), East Africa Light Battery, "Rekkies", Supply and Transport, the East African Engineers (EAE), A small number had gone into the RAF.

The call for KR men across the entire East African Command (EAC)—even to the point of needing its colonel for greater things—reduced it so completely that by the end of 1940 it was no longer recognisable. It existed as a training depot for recruits from any part of the world. By mid-1941, maintaining the organization was no longer economic, the KR closed down and was not reactivated until 1950.

Throughout all the preparation for war and the transfer of men in all directions, the KDF remained a constant. Formed as the original 'Burgher Army' in 1927, the KDF was never disbanded, and its existence reaffirmed by ordnance in 1937, from which time it was a parallel battalion to the KR. De facto, the KR and KDF were treated as two battalions of the same regiment and transfers between the two were not uncommon. The big difference was, unlike the KR, the KDF was not deployed outside of Kenya. The KDF's non-combatant role spanned the spectrum of activities demanded by the war, especially in the fields of administration and transportation.

Men of the KDF were dispersed into a huge pool of units such as the East African Military Labour Corps, East African Army Service Corps, East African Army Ordnance Corps, East African Army Medical Corps, East African Army Education Corps, East African Intelligence Corps, East African Engineers and African Pioneer Corps (East African).

In a nutshell, the KR was an infantry-officer pool for the KAR, which could be sent anywhere in the world. The KDF was confined to Kenya, or very close by, and was involved in non-combat roles. In all, over 3,500 members of the KR joined the East African forces. Of these, more than 1,500 were commissioned as officers in the KAR battalions of Kenya, Uganda, Tanganyika and Nyasaland, and in the Northern Rhodesia Regiment.

At Nanyuki on August 26, 1939, 5KAR received orders for mobilisation for a global conflict that was now deemed imminent. The process ran smoothly. The Colours and officers' mess silver were taken to a Nairobi bank for safekeeping. Reinforcements of officers and NCOs, drawn for the most part from the Kenya Regiment, arrived by the end of the month.

The mobilisation plan, in the event of hostilities with Italy, visualised 5KAR moving to a battle station in the Isiolo area. Accordingly, on September 2, the battalion left Nanyuki by road transport for Isiolo.

This transport was almost entirely commandeered: African and Indian buses and trucks, most in a dubious state of repair. The vehicles came straight off the roads and were given a quick inspection by overworked MT personnel. If it was felt they could make the distance to Isiolo, the vehicles were employed. Most made the trip, and some even remained with the battalion throughout the campaign.

"D" Company was deployed along the Northern Frontier, to Wajir, Moyale and Mandera, while a platoon from "C" Company was posted to Garissa on the eastern border with Italian Somaliland to protect the aerodrome. However, it would be nine months before Italy entered the war, and "C" Company was moved to reoccupy Moyale.

The Allies now waited for the anticipated Italian offensive which, it was believed, had close on 50 brigades in East Africa. Battalion Headquarters and two companies were garrisoned at Isiolo, while one company was at Wajir and a fourth at Moyale. Before long, though, 5KAR, less the two forward companies, retired to Nanyuki for further combat exercises.

During these exercises the askari of the KAR were put into boots for the first time in their history. It was generally held this was a mistake, that it would slow them up, that they would get soft feet, and so on. In fact it was a very wise order and, although at first there were a number of blistered feet, it very soon turned out that foot casualties from thorns and stones were completely eliminated and there was no apparent loss of speed across country.

Directly after the exercises, 5KAR was stationed once again at Isiolo, which saved it a 50-mile march back to Nanyuki. From there all non-regular officers were posted to the second course at the recently established "School of Instruction" at Nakuru for further general training. At this time, the 1st, 2nd and 6th KAR battalions had moved up to Kenya. At Nanyuki, 5KAR doubled up in its quarters to accommodate 6KAR.

The Allied force in East Africa was now beginning to take shape. The 22nd Mountain Battery from India had arrived, and troops from the Gold Coast and from South Africa were preparing to sail. The KAR itself was expanding fast, and ancillary units such as the East African Reconnaissance Squadron, the East African Light Battery, and medical and transport units had been formed. From Southern Rhodesia came an armoured car unit, the Southern Rhodesia Armoured Car Regiment. Stores and equipment of all kinds were arriving from the United Kingdom and from South Africa.

As the rains abated and the roads to the north dried out, 5KAR, with the bulk of the brigade, moved north and occupied the wells at Arbo, just south of Wajir. There it remained, practising "bush warfare" until the Italians declared war in June 1940·

By the time Italy invaded British Somaliland on August 2, 1940, the Kenyan Southern Front, under Lieutenant General Sir Alan Cunningham

DSO, MC, had been built up to three divisions, numbering 115,000 troops:

1. 1st South African Division, Major-General George Brink DSO
2. 11th African Division, Major-General Harry Wetherall DSO, MC
3. 12th African Division, Major-General Reade Godwin-Austen OBE, MC (1940–1941); Major-General Charles Christopher Fowkes (1941–1943)

When Italy declared war on Britain and France on June 10, 1940, Prince Amedeo, 3rd Duke of Aosta became the Commander-in-Chief of Italian East African Armed Forces (*Comando Forze Armate dell'Africa Orientale Italiana*). Numbering 250,000 troops, the force comprised three corps and one division:

1. Northern Sector, in Asmara, Lieutenant-General Luigi Frusci (Italian Eritrea)
2. Southern Sector, in Gimma, General Pietro Gazzera
3. Eastern Sector, in Addis Ababa, General Guglielmo Nasi
4. Giuba Sector, in Mogadishu, Lieutenant-General Carlo De Simone (Southern Italian Somaliland)

The British Offensive

In North Africa, General Archibald Wavell, Commander-in-Chief Middle East, was about to launch his campaign against the Italians on the Egyptian border. As part of his plan, he directed that, in Kenya, the East African Forces should close the gap between them and the enemy and regain the initiative prior to a general advance.

There then followed a dramatic event which was to have an immense effect on the whole conduct of the Abyssinian Campaign. Major-General Godwin-Austin, commanding the 12th African Division, and fresh from the evacuation of British Somaliland, sensing that his troops had been on the defensive for too long, decided that, as a preliminary, he must stage a decisive victory to restore the offensive spirit.

He proposed therefore to launch the best part of his command against Buna, 70 miles south of Moyale. 5KAR, being at that time at Marsabit to the west, were left to maintain a presence in that sector. Detailed plans, including air reconnaissance and special maps, were prepared, but a little more than a fortnight before the date of the proposed operation the Italians evacuated the division's objective.

The plan was then immediately switched to an attack on El Wak, 100 miles to the east. Previously attacked by 5KAR and 1KAR, an officer from 5KAR, serving temporarily with divisional staff, was detailed to cut out of the bush roads and tracks leading to the El Wak position. On this "practice course" as many of the troops as possible were exercised, and on December 16, the attack was launched.

The Italians, believing that nothing more than a battalion could possibly reach them, were taken completely by surprise and totally overwhelmed by the attack of the two brigades supported by aircraft, artillery, tanks and armoured cars. Apart from 15 artillery pieces and around 100 prisoners,

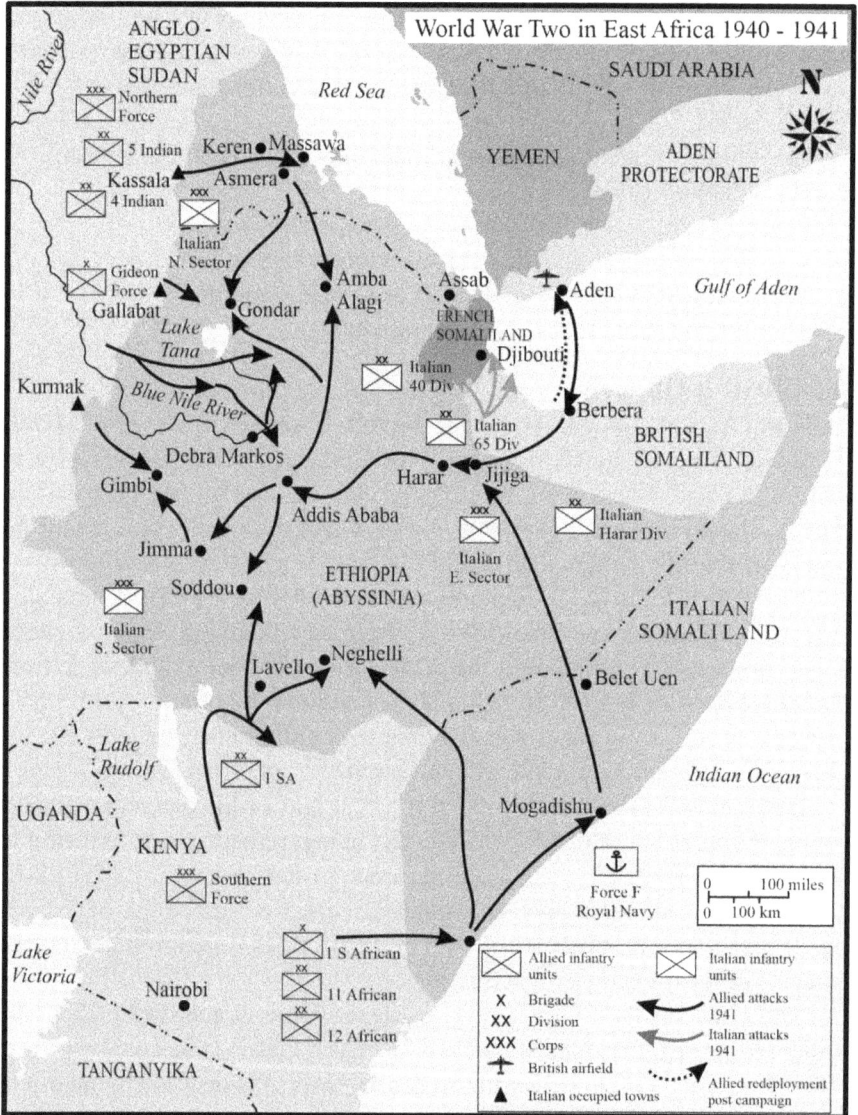

World War Two in East Africa 1940 - 1941

valuable secret documents, including the cypher books and general defence plan for Italian Somaliland, were captured.

This swift and sudden disaster to the enemy force appeared to destroy their morale, particularly as the battalion stationed at El Wak was one of many similar colonial infantry battalions on which they were relying for the defence of Italian Somaliland. As a result the enemy withdrew all their forces, except the Afmadu garrison behind the line of the Juba River, and in the end made little or no attempt to stem the advance of the East African Force. On the side of the East African forces the plan to close the gap gave way to that of a more immediate general advance.

In February 1941, General Cunningham's Southern Force launched a two-pronged attack across the northern and eastern borders of Kenya, at the start of a 2,000-mile advance which broke Italian power in East Africa. At the same time, the Northern Force under General Platt invaded Italian-occupied Eritrea and western Abyssinia.

On April 6, 1941, a mixed column from Cunningham's right pincer, the 11th African Division, formed up on the outskirts of Addis Ababa for the triumphal entry. First the war correspondents, who had suddenly appeared at Adama, were allowed to go on ahead. Then a party consisting of "C" Squadron, East Africa Armoured Car Regiment, followed by Brigadier Fowkes and advance parties of the 1st South African Brigade. They were followed by the South African armoured cars, General Wetherall, General Officer Commanding 11 Division, and Brigadier Dan Pienaar, commanding the 1st South African Infantry Brigade. Finally, 22 Bde Headquarters, 5KAR (less "B" and "C" Coys left at Adama), a company of 6KAR, the 22nd Indian Mountain Battery', a detachment from 5 South African Anti-aircraft Battery, and a platoon from 3KAR.

From the liberated capital, 23 Nigerian Brigade and 22 East Africa Brigade marched west and south to bring an end to the campaign. In July, Italian General Gazzera finally capitulated. The Allies now turned their attention to Madagascar.

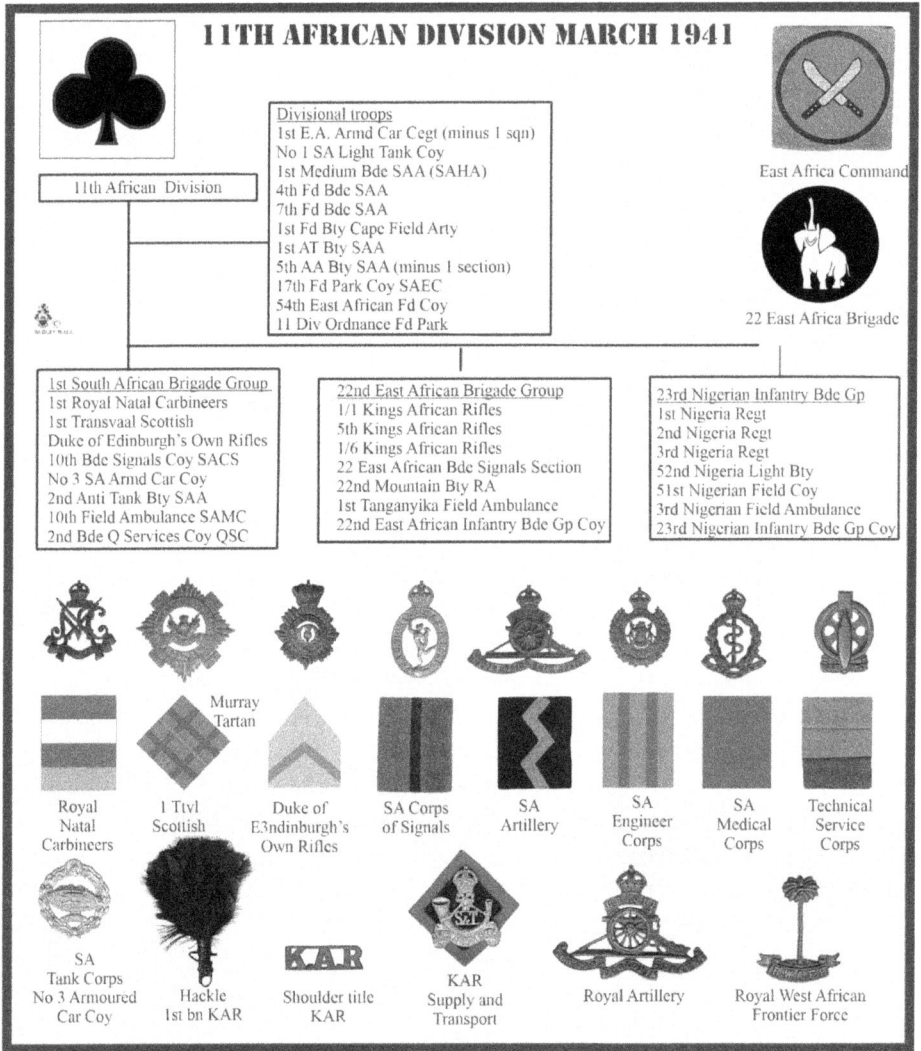

18

11TH AFRICAN DIVISION MARCH 1941

11th African Division

East Africa Command

22 East Africa Brigade

Divisional troops
1st E.A. Armd Car Cegt (minus 1 sqn)
No 1 SA Light Tank Coy
1st Medium Bde SAA (SAHA)
4th Fd Bde SAA
7th Fd Bde SAA
1st Fd Bty Cape Field Arty
1st AT Bty SAA
5th AA Bty SAA (minus 1 section)
17th Fd Park Coy SAEC
54th East African Fd Coy
11 Div Ordnance Fd Park

1st South African Brigade Group
1st Royal Natal Carbineers
1st Transvaal Scottish
Duke of Edinburgh's Own Rifles
10th Bde Signals Coy SACS
No 3 SA Armd Car Coy
2nd Anti Tank Bty SAA
10th Field Ambulance SAMC
2nd Bde Q Services Coy QSC

22nd East African Brigade Group
1/1 Kings African Rifles
5th Kings African Rifles
1/6 Kings African Rifles
22 East African Bde Signals Section
22nd Mountain Bty RA
1st Tanganyika Field Ambulance
22nd East African Infantry Bde Gp Coy

23rd Nigerian Infantry Bde Gp
1st Nigeria Regt
2nd Nigeria Regt
3rd Nigeria Regt
52nd Nigeria Light Bty
51st Nigerian Field Coy
3rd Nigerian Field Ambulance
23rd Nigerian Infantry Bde Gp Coy

Royal Natal Carbineers | 1 Ttvl Scottish (Murray Tartan) | Duke of E3ndinburgh's Own Rifles | SA Corps of Signals | SA Artillery | SA Engineer Corps | SA Medical Corps | Technical Service Corps

SA Tank Corps No 3 Armoured Car Coy | Hackle 1st bn KAR | Shoulder title KAR | KAR Supply and Transport | Royal Artillery | Royal West African Frontier Force

12TH AFRICAN DIVISION 1940 - MARCH 1941

12th African Division

Divisional troops
B Sqn 1st EA Armd Car Regt
1st Fd Bty Cape Field Arty
2nd AT Bty SAA
1 section 6th AA Bty SAA
19th Fd Park Coy SAEC
1 coy 1/3 KAR machine guns (- 1 pl)
12 Div Ordnance Fd Park
No 1 Irregular Coy
Det no 4 Irregular Coy

Gold Coast Regiment

GCR RWAFF

Gold Coast Regiment
Shoulder title

East Africa Command

1st South Africa Brigade Group
1st Royal Natal Carbineers
1st Transvaal Scottish
Duke of Edinburgh's Own Rifles
10th Bde Signals Coy SACS
No 3 SA Armd Car Coy
4 Fd Bde SAA (10,11,12 fd btys)
1st Fd Coy SAEC
1 Bde Q Services Coy
10 Fd Ambulance SAMC
No 1 Mobile Genl Wksps TSC

22nd East African Brigade Group
1/1 Kings African Rifles
1/5 Kings African Rifles
1/6 Kings African Rifles
22 East African Bde Signals Section
22nd Mountain Bty Indian Arty
54th East Africa Fd Coy
22 East Africa Bde Gp Coy
1st Tanganyika Field Ambulance

24th Gold Coast Inf Bde Gp
1st Gold Coast Regt
2nd Gold Coast Regt
3rd Gold Coast Rregt
51st Gold Coast Light Bty
52nd Gold Coast Fd Coy
4th Gold Coast Fd Ambulance
24 Gold Coast Inf Bde Gp Coy

Royal Natal Carbineers	1 Tvl Scottish	Dukes	SA Corps of Signals	SA Armd Cars	SA Arty	SA Engineer Corps	"Q" Services Corps	SA Medical Corps	Technical Service Corps

Murray Tartan

EA Command was raised on 15th September 1941 as a British formation to deal with. the threat from the various Italian territories in East Africa. Under command were 22 EA Bde and 25 EA Bde. These two Bdes were allocated to 12th African Division commanded by Maj Gen Fowkes. SA troops were also attached to form the third Bde of this division. Elements of the support services were drawn from local units manned by both white and black East Africans. These personnel were in locally raised units that consisted of the following:
East African Armoured Corps
East African Artillery
East African Engineers
East African Survey Unit
East African Signal Corps
East African Army Service Corps (logistics / supply/transport)
East African Army Medical Corps
East African Army ordnance Corps

Hat flashes of some east African units

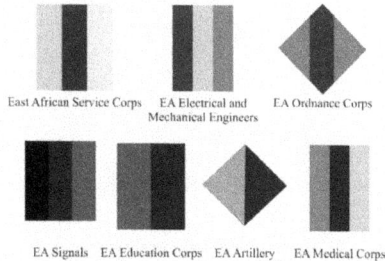

East African Service Corps   EA Electrical and Mechanical Engineers   EA Ordnance Corps

EA Signals   EA Education Corps   EA Artillery   EA Medical Corps

Kenya Defence Force

East Africa Army Service Corps

EA Electrical and Mechanical Engineers

EA Army Medical Corps

1st Nairobi Bn KDF

Kenya Regiment

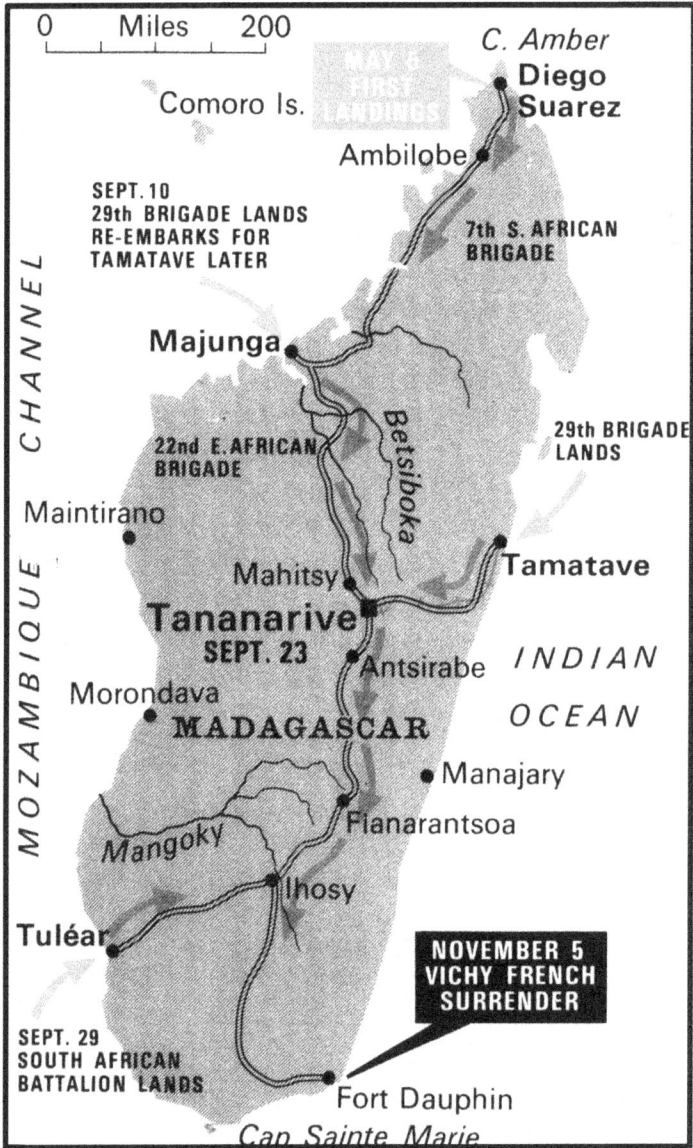

```
0    Miles   200

                              C. Amber
          Comoro Is.         Diego
                             Suarez
MAY 5                Ambilobe
FIRST
LANDINGS

SEPT.10
29th BRIGADE LANDS
RE-EMBARKS FOR          7th S.AFRICAN
TAMATAVE LATER          BRIGADE

Majunga

              Betsiboka

22nd E.AFRICAN              29th BRIGADE
BRIGADE                    LANDS

Maintirano
                    Mahitsy       Tamatave
           Tananarive
           SEPT. 23    Antsirabe    INDIAN
Morondava
           MADAGASCAR              OCEAN

                        Manajary
Mangoky          Fianarantsoa
            Ihosy
Tuléar                   NOVEMBER 5
                         VICHY FRENCH
                         SURRENDER
SEPT. 29
SOUTH AFRICAN
BATTALION LANDS   Fort Dauphin
            Cap Sainte Marie
```

Madagascar Invasion

The 300-mile wide Mozambique Channel separating Madagascar from the east African coast was a major shipping route which, lying as it did between neutral Portuguese East Africa (now Mozambique) and the supposedly neutral French Vichy Madagascar, provided an excellent hunting ground for Japanese submarines. Repeated attacks on British shipping indicated Diego Suarez was being used as a base for these hostile craft. In view of the importance of the supply lines to Egypt and India it was essential to ensure that Madagascar should stop being used by the enemy. Moreover, the possession of Diego Suarez, in conjunction with Colombo and Mombasa, would provide the British navy with a good strategic triangle for defending the Indian Ocean. When efforts to achieve these objectives by negotiation failed, because of the strong German influence over Vichy, there remained only one option: invasion.

The fleet for Operation Ironclad, the seizure of the port of Diego-Suarez (now Antsiranana) included the battleship HMS *Ramillies*, the carrier HMS *Illustrious*, the cruisers HMS *Hermione* and HMS *Devonshire*, 11 destroyers, minesweepers, corvettes and 15 assault ships. The 13th and 15th Infantry Brigades of the 5th Division and the 29th Independent Infantry Brigade destined for India were diverted to Madagascar.

Ironclad, which was the largest amphibious operation for British forces since the Dardanelles campaign in World War One, was directed at Diego Suarez, where the first assault went in at 4.30 a.m. on 5 May 1942. Two days later the fighting ceased with the harbour forts in the Diego Suarez Bay in British hands.

It was then decided to occupy the whole island, but Vichy French Governor General of Madagascar, Armand Annet, and his military commander, General Guillemet, resisted and chose to fight, holding out as long as they could.

On June 3, 1942, the 22nd East African Brigade, which had played such an exemplary role in the Abyssinian Campaign, set sail from Mombasa on the SS *Winchester Castle*. The infantry comprised 5 (Kenya) KAR, 1/1 (Nyasaland) KAR and 1/6 (Tanganyika) KAR. The brigade was now commanded by Brigadier William Alfred Dimoline OBE, MC, after Fowkes had been promoted to major-general and placed in command of 12 Division

Early in September 1943, three British convoys, totalling over 50 vessels, came together south of Mayotte. This large fleet, carrying troops, transport and stores made its way to the chosen destination nine miles north of Majunga on the island's west coast where it anchored before midnight. At this time, with the attachment of 29th Brigade, South African 7th Motorised Brigade and Rhodesian 27th Infantry Brigade, 22 Brigade effectively became a brigade group.

After 22 Brigade disembarked at Majunga, 29 Brigade was shipped to the east coast port of Tamatave. The two brigades captured Tananarive and then set off southward to clear the rest of the island. A week later, the South African Battalion landed at Tulear to support the cordon, and on November 5, the Vichy French surrendered at Fort Dauphin.

**Lieutenant-General Douglas Povah Dickinson
CB, DSO, OBE, MC**
(NPG Academic Licence)

Born on November 6, 1886, Douglas Povah Dickinson was commissioned into the Welch Regiment in 1906, and served in World War One in France and Belgium. He was subsequently appointed Deputy Assistant Quartermaster-General at the Staff College, Camberley, in 1925, Inspector of the Iraqi Army in Kurdistan in 1930, and Inspector with the British Military Mission attached to the Iraqi Army in 1932.

He went on to be Commanding Officer of the 1st Battalion of The Welch Regiment in 1934, Commandant of the Nigeria Regiment in 1936 and Inspector-General of the African Colonial Forces early in 1939. Dickinson served in World War Two as General Officer Commanding the East Africa Force from September 1939, and as Chief of Staff of Western Command from January 1941. He retired in 1944, and died on January 8, 1949, aged 62.

During his military career, General Dickinson was appointed a Commander of the Order of the Bath (1941), a Companion of the Distinguished Service Order (1917), and an Officer of the Order of the British Empire (1933). He was also awarded the Military Cross for bravery (1916), the Iraqi Order of Al Rafidain, Third Class (1933), and the American Bronze Star Medal (1947).

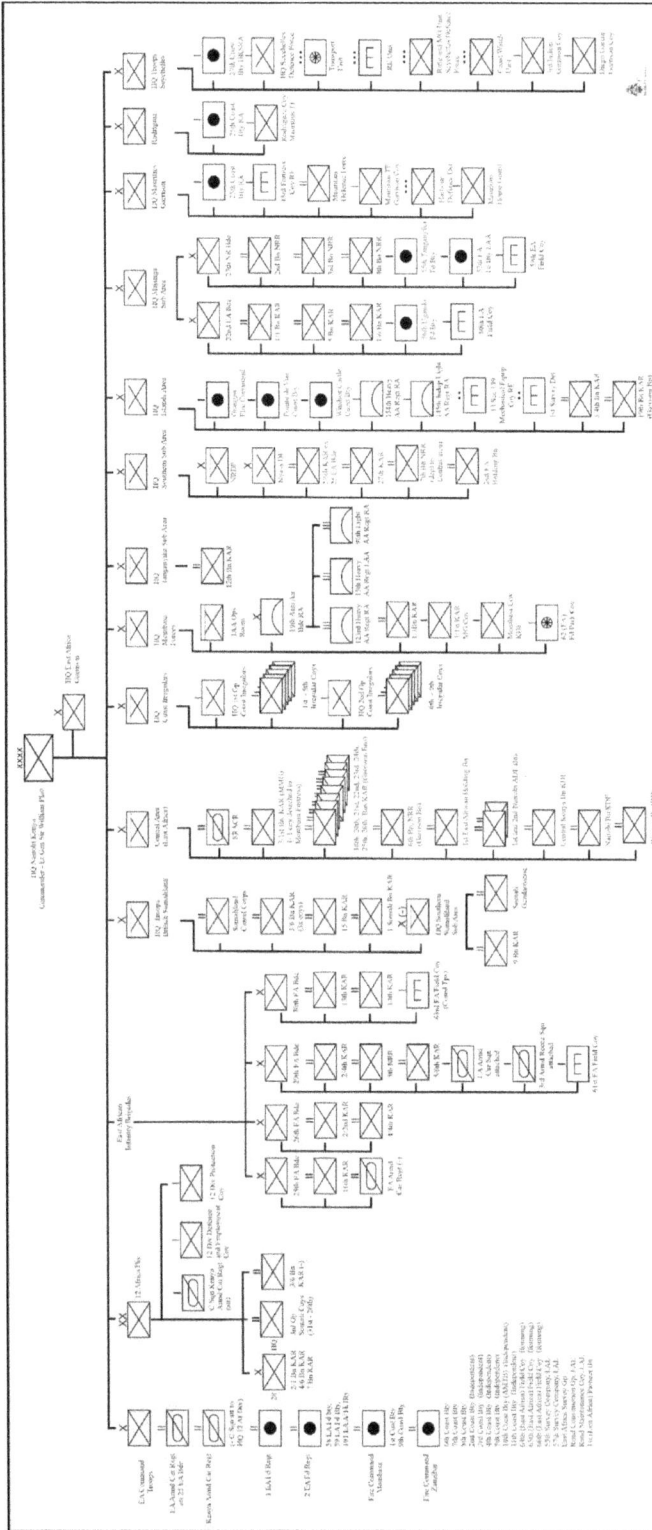

See gweaa.com for larger version

Despatch

At the end of December 1939, Dickinson submitted the following despatch to the Under Secretary of State at the War Office, John Lyttelton, his first since his appointment as General Officer Commanding the Forces in East Africa in August. He details his thorough preparations and the situation in East Africa in the four-month-old war.

The original copy of the Despatch can be found at The National Archives, London, WO 276/378. In the following pages, the layout of the original document has been retained.

Abbreviations

A Branch – Administrative Branch
AA – Assistant Adjutant
ADOS – Assistant Division Signal Officer
ADS & T – Assistant Director Supply & Transport
Bn – Battalion
CB – Companion of the Order of the Bath
Coy – Company
CP – Command Post
CRA – Chief Royal Artillery
CRE – Chief Royal Engineer
DJAG – Deputy Judge Advocate General
DSO – Distinguished Service Order
EAASC – East Africa Army Service Corps
EAE – East African Engineers
GRO – General Routine Order
GSGS – Geographical Section, General Staff (MI 4)
KAR – King's African Rifles
KC – King's Counsel
KCB – Knight Commander of the Order of the Bath
KCMG – Knight Commander of the Order of St Michael and St George
KCVO – Knight Commander of the Royal Victorian Order

KDF – Kenya Defence Force
KUR & H – Kenya & Uganda Railways and Harbours
L of C – Lines of Communication
MC – Military Cross
MT / MMT – Motor/Mechanised Transport / Motor Mechanic Transport
NCO / BNCO – Non-commissioned officer / British Non-commissioned officer
NFD – Northern Frontier District
ODC – Oversea Defence Committee
PWD – Public Works Department
Q Branch – Quartermaster Branch
QMG – Quartermaster general
RA – Royal Artillery
RAF / SRAF – Royal Air Force / Squadron Royal Air Force
RARO – Regular Army Reserve of Officers
TA – Territorial Army
TT – Territorial Transport
W/T – Wireless Telegraph
YMCA – Young Men's Christian Association

EAST AFRICA FORCE

DESPATCH No. 1

Distribution List

1.	}	
2.	}	**Under Secretary of Sate,**
3.	}	**The War Office**
4.	}	
5.	}	
6.	}	
7.	}	
8.	}	**Chief Political Liaison Officer**
9.	}	
10.	}	
11.	}	
12.	}	**Minister of Defence,**
		Southern Rhodesia
13.	}	
to	}	**Spare**
18	}	

FILE NO. CREAF 8/800,
SECRET
HEADQUARTERS, EAST AFRICA FORCE,
NAIROBI,
31st December 1939

The Under Secretary of State
The War Office
Whitehall, S.W.1

Sir;

It may be of interest to the Army
Council to receive a comprehensive report of the
activities of East Africa Force from the commencement
of the war, and a description of the present military
situation in East Africa. I have, therefore, the
honour to address to you my first despatch since the
outbreak of war.

2.　　　　I arrived in East Africa, (Nairobi),
as Inspector General, African Colonial Forces,
accompanied by my Staff Officer, Lt.-Colonel W. H. A.
Bishop on the 22nd August, 1939, to commence a normal
inspection tour of the King's African Rifles in the
East African Territories and of the Northern Rhodesia
Regiment. My itinerary also included a visit to Southern
Rhodesia. On my way to Nairobi I had had the opportunity
of carrying out conversations with the General Officer
Commanding in Chief, Middle East, at Cairo, and at
Khartoum, with His Excellency the Governor General of
the Sudan, and the General Officer Commanding troops in
the Sudan. On my arrival at Nairobi it was apparent
that war with Germany and Italy was imminent. I
therefore applied myself to investigating the local
defence/

/defence situation, I received the telegram informing me that I had been appointed General Officer Commanding the Forces in East Africa on the 31st August, and the Telegram informing me that war had broken out with Germany on the 3rd September.

3.   The plan of operations in the event of war with Germany and/or Italy was contained in Oversea Defence Committee Memorandum No, 700 M. Further details were included in the defence schemes of the Northern and Southern Brigades, the King's African Rifles and the Northern Rhodesia Regiment. My first responsibility, on assuming command of the military forces in East Africa was, therefore, the implementing of the arrangements set out under "precautionary" and "war" stages in O.D.C. Memorandum No 700 M. The preliminary moves laid down in that Memorandum were carried into effect. Details of these and subsequent operational moves are given in the summary of my war diary which is at Appendix "A".

                    The few troops available for the Defence of Kenya at the outbreak of war, should Italy join Germany made the rapid collection and internment of all the Germans in Kenya and Tanganyika of paramount Importance. Plans had been prepared before the war, and worked well in all Territories. In view of the magnitude of the task which faced the civil and military authorities, particularly in Tanganyika, I consider that great credit due for the smooth and efficient manner in which the plans were carried out. No arrangements had, however, been made by the military authorities in Kenya for the apprehension of any German nationals who might seek to evade the measures taken in Tanganyika for their internment by/

3

/by moving across the frontier between that Territory and Kenya. It was also possible that these individuals might have received instructions from their own Government to do all in their power to create a diversion on the southern frontier of Kenya with the object of assisting an Italian advance from the north. I was therefore obliged to extemporise arrangements for the guarding of the frontier between Kenya and Tanganyika. The personnel who carried out this duty were members of the Kenya Defence Force, and on receipt of their instructions they moved to their posts with commendable despatch.

4.   The operational moves referred to above, and the maintenance of the troops in their war stations was gravely handicapped by a shortage of transport. War establishments for the East Africa Army Service Corps had been worked out before the war, based on the organisation being built up on the Supply and Transport Corps, K.A.R. which existed in time of peace. This Corps, however, provided a totally inadequate nucleus for the wartime supply and transport organisation. Furthermore, no legislation existed in the East African Territories under which any military unit other than battalions of the King's African Rifles, the Kenya Regiment and the Kenya Defence Force could legally be formed, commanded and administered, although the various units enumerated in O.D.C. Memorandum 700 M., and to be formed on the outbreak of war, had been agreed to by all Territories. The rates of pay for drivers authorised in time of peace were found to be inadequate to obtain the very large number required in war without resource to compulsion/

/compulsion, which was obviously undesirable. The vast majority of the vehicles in all the East Africa Territories was in a very bad state of repair. For these reasons, the very greatest difficulty was encountered, and is still being encountered, in the mobilisation of the supply and transport organisation. Further details are given in Appendix "B",

I found the shortage of tentage, stores, weapons (especially for anti-tank defence) and ammunition to be so serious that I cabled War Office and Army Headquarters India for permission to obtain my essential requirements from India. I desire to record my appreciation of the prompt and satisfactory manner in which Army Headquarters India met these very urgent demands so far as was in their power directly War Office financial authority was received.

5. Force Headquarters.

The extent to which the peace establishment of the Forces in East Africa had to be expanded on mobilisation made it imperative to employ the very few Regular Officers available, for training and leading fighting Units. Consequently, with the exception of 7 Regular Officers including Heads of Services, who came out from the United Kingdom for the purpose, I have had to form my Headquarters Staff by employing Officers of the Regular Army Reserve of Officers, and others who had served in the Great War of 1914-18, and who are too old to serve with Units in the field. With one exception none of these officers have had any previous Staff experience whatever. For clerks I have had to depend entirely on women as it has been/

5

/been impossible to find men to do this work, The difficulties which arose in organising my Headquarters in these circumstances, and, in training the organisation to work smoothly and efficiently, will be appreciated. I have had to contend with the same difficulties in forming my Headquarters Line of Communications, and the Area Headquarters in each Territory over which my Command extends.

One result of this situation has been that I have experienced considerable difficulty obtaining control over expenditure. This question is dealt with more fully in the several Appendices to this Despatch. Arrangements were made for the organisation of an intelligence system throughout East Africa as quickly as possible, and for the co-ordination of intelligence activities between East Africa, the Sudan and Egypt. An Intelligence Corps was also organised in the Northern Frontier District. Further information regarding Intelligence, Survey and Cipher activities is given in Appendix "C",

The collection of information regarding any possible Internal Security troubles throughout the area is largely in the hands of the Criminal Investigation Departments of the various Territories. The successful rounding up of the Germans in all the East African Territories, including Tanganyika where trouble had been anticipated, had a good effect on the native mind Generally speaking, the attitude of native opinion throughout East Africa is most satisfactory. Many individuals who might have menaced internal security and stirred up trouble amongst the native populations are now in internment camps. Only those Germans who are not/

6

not considered dangerous are on parole. The Criminal
Investigation Departments also keep a constant watch
on Italian and other possible enemy agents, and on native
and Indian affairs. These departments have been of
considerable assistance to me in checking leakages of
official information, of which there were certain
instances in the early days of the war.

6.   Arrangements had been made before the
war for the Officers and British Warrant and Non-Commissioned
Officers required to complete existing units to war
establishment, and to fill vacancies in new units authorised
in O.D.C. Memorandum 700 M., to be drawn from the Kenya
Regiment. No arrangements had, however, been made for
the utilisation of the large numbers of R.A.R.O. resident
in East Africa. and particularly in Kenya. The young
men from the Kenya Regiment, though admirable material,
had received very little training indeed at the outbreak
of war, and the posting of large numbers of these untrained
European personnel to K.A.R. battalions had an adverse
effect on the morale of the trained African soldiers and
on the efficiency of the units. I therefore sought
permission to form an Officers Instructional School, at
which as many as possible of these potential officers and
N.C.O.'s are now undergoing an intensive three months
course of training. Those for whom vacancies could not
be found at the School have been removed from their
Companies and are undergoing courses of training organised
under unit arrangements. When these young men attain the
Standard prescribed for the Officer's Efficiency Test,
(vide Appendix XXXII Territorial Army Regulations), they
are promoted, in order of merit, to fill Officer and N.C.O.
vacancies in the establishment of units.

7

7.   <u>Engineering.</u>

The situation regarding engineering
staff and work is set out in full in Appendix "E". I
would, however, emphasise the fact that my task in
ensuring that the large amount of engineering work
immediately necessary on the outbreak of war was carried
out expeditiously and economically was mainly complicated
by the total absence of any engineering staff or units.
The situation is, however, now considerably more satisfactory
in this respect.

8.   <u>Survey.</u>   The provision of survey units in the
African Colonial Forces had been under the consideration
of myself and my predecessor in the Colonial Office before
the war, and plans had been prepared, in consultation
with M.I. 4. at the War Office and the Survey Departments
in the Territories concerned, for the formation of
Survey Companies in East and West Africa. A few days
after the war the 1st East Africa Field Survey Company
was formed. The unit moved up to the Northern Frontier
District on the 16th September, and commenced the mapping
of certain portions of this vast area which are of
particular military importance. The map reproduction
section is stationed at Dar-es-Salaam.

I received an offer from the Southern
Rhodesia Government on the 1st November for the employment
of a Field Survey Company which had been raised in their
Territory.

I have sought permission from the
War Office to accept this offer from the Southern
Rhodesia Government, but this authority has not, up to
the present, been communicated to me.

Further details regarding map
reproduction/

8

/reproduction and the supply of maps are at Appendix "D".

9. Signals.   The situation regarding Signals is given in detail in Appendix "F". Telegraphic and telephonic communications were poor and quite inadequate at the outbreak of war. Most of the W/T Sets of the Army were employed in permanent stations in the Northern Frontier District, and it was not till the end of September, when Force Headquarters Signals arrived, that any satisfactory communications were established in this Command.

10. Artillery.
                  Prior to the arrival of the 22nd Mountain Battery Royal Artillery from India on 11th September, 1939, there were no guns whatever in this country.
                  The 1st East Africa Light Battery was formed on 21st September and its training carried out with the assistance of instructors and equipment of 22nd Mountain Battery R.A. The further training of this Battery is being retarded through lack of equipment.
                  As soon as 1st East Africa Light Battery receives its equipment I propose to appoint Major J.C. D'Arcy, R.A., now commanding 22nd Mountain Battery, C.R.A. to the East Africa Force.

11. Reconnaissance Squadron.
                  Immediately prior to the outbreak of war the Kenya Government was authorised to raise an Armoured Car Company. As there was little prospect of obtaining armoured cars from elsewhere, and armour plating was unobtainable, I decided to raise instead a Reconnaissance Squadron./

9.

/Squadron. This Unit consists of a Headquarters and three Troops, each of two sections, each of two fighting cars. The vehicles are Ford one-ton trucks with mountings to take a Bren gun on the cab and the tail to fire in any direction. The crew of each car consists of two men and a driver, and armament one Bren gun and two rifles. Each section is organised as to be completely self contained.

I would stress the fact that this Reconnaissance Squadron is the only Unit available for reconnaissance duties in the East Africa Force.

12. Machine Gun Battalion.

In view of the suitability of much of the country in the Northern Frontier District for the employment of machine guns, and the paucity of my Force in relation to the extent of the area to be defended, I have re-organised the 3rd Battalion K.A.R. as a machine gun Battalion. This has been effected by the transfer to this battalion of trained machine gunners and machine gun equipment from other battalions.

It will be recalled that, under the pre-war scheme of re-organisation of the African Colonial Forces, the machine gun platoons in battalions have been replaced by mortar platoons. Until, however, the mortar equipment became available, battalions retained platoons equipped with machine guns. It has, therefore, been possible to effect this re-organisation without any additional expenditure. To save man-power I am experimenting with using donkeys for carrying the machine guns, and have obtained a hardy type locally for the purpose. These donkeys can be transported by M.T. if the need/

10.

/need to do so should arise.

13. <u>Air</u>.

On the outbreak of war, No. 223
Squadron, Royal Air Force, was removed, in accordance with
the pre-war plan, from Nairobi to the Sudan. Owing to
the promptitude with which the Southern Rhodesia
Government despatched No. 1. Squadron, Southern Rhodesia
Air Force, to Nairobi, I was not entirely bereft of any
form of air co-operation. This Squadron was, however,
on a cadre basis, and is only now being brought up to
full squadron establishment.

Certain Auxiliary Air Units for coast
watching and intercommunication duties were formed from
the civil aircraft companies operating in East Africa.
Details are given in the memorandum at Appendix "J".

14. The pre-war defence plan in Kenya was
to hold the line of the Tana and the Uaso-Nyiro Rivers
from Garsen to Archer's Post (vide map attached, Appendix
"G"). This plan was, I consider, the best that could be
devised in view of the fact that there were only two
Battalions available at the outset of war. As, however,
time has allowed of the concentration of additional
K.A.R. Battalions and other units in Kenya, vide
Location Statement at Appendix "H", I have modified the
plan with the object of hampering any possible Italian
advance through the Northern Frontier District by
denying as long as possible the main sources of water
at Wajir and Moyale. A reserve position, running along
the eastern and north-eastern slopes of the Kenya
Highlands has also been reconnoitred. Arrangements
have been made to strengthen the foremost defended
localities by the erection of tactical wire obstacles,
the revetment of trenches, and the construction of a/

11

/a certain number of concrete pill-boxes. This work has been carried out under the direction, and with the assistance of the 1st East Africa Engineer Company, which has been formed since the outbreak of war.

My principal problem in organising the defensive system in the Northern Frontier District has been the difficulty of providing any satisfactory defence against an attack supported by tanks. I have no anti-tank artillery, and very few anti-tank rifles. Furthermore, except in the south, along the lower reaches of the River Tana, there are no natural anti-tank obstacles that I can utilise. Owing to the few troops available and the wide extent of country over which I can be attacked, all my defensive positions can be out-flanked comparatively easily. Although I am making the foremost defended localities to be occupied by the infantry as strong as possible, my plan of defence is to oppose any advance from Abyssinia or Italian Somaliland with the minimum force necessary to impose delay, keeping the remainder as fluid and mobile as possible to use as opportunity offers. I am investigating the possibility of constructing anti-tank mines locally.

Another difficulty has been the lack of any roads in the Northern Frontier District other than sandy tracks which become completely impassable during the rainy seasons. I have been allotted the sum of £50,000 by the War Office for the improvement of communications within this area. I am endeavouring to obtain what I consider to be the best possible value for the expenditure of this money by concentrating on:-

(a) The provision of all-weather roads from the potential rail head at Nanyuki to the sites selected for/

12

/for the various rail head depots.

(b)   The construction of an all-weather road from Nanyuki to Archer's Post.

(c)   The improvement, so far as funds permit, of the road from Isiolo to Wajir.

I am utilising the two Pioneer Battalions, whose formation was authorised by the War Office, on this work, and I have also engaged the services of a civilian construction company, whose experience and plant are proving most valuable. As there is insufficient money to improve the existing tracks in the northern Frontier District to such an extent as to ensure the possibility of maintaining troops at any period of the year in the foremost defended localities which I consider tactically desirable to defend, I have stored a reserve of food, ammunition, etc., at those localities.

Considerable progress has been made in the investigation and development of water supplies throughout the operational area. The provision of the requisite supplies of water for the troops occupying the defensive positions in the Northern Frontier District is a particularly difficult problem. I have been very fortunate in obtaining, through the generosity of the Governments of Southern Rhodesia and Uganda, the loan of the services of expert technicians to assist me in the solution of this problem. The prosecution of this work is now awaiting authority from the War Office for certain expenditure on plant required for the construction of wells and boreholes. On receipt of the necessary authority, the work will be carried out by the water section of the East Africa Engineer Company, assisted by the Pioneers. /

13

15.　　　　　Before leaving London, I received
instructions to investigate, on my arrival in East Africa,
the possibility of organising an advance into Italian East
Africa from Kenya in the event of Italy entering the war
against us. The result of my investigations was
communicated to the War Office. Owing to the administrative difficulties, I was ordered to abandon the project,
and to study the question of employing small mobile
columns to harass the Italians in the Southern part of
Abyssinia. As the result of a meeting with the General
Officer Commanding in Chief, Middle East, at Khartoum, I
have prepared plans for the provision of a Colonial Division
to be drawn from East, Central and West Africa, with a
view to its subsequent employment as required by the War
Office.

　　　　　These plans have been forwarded to the
War Office through the General Officer Commanding in Chief,
Middle East.

　　　　　I am arranging a Staff Exercise at
Mombasa to study the embarkation and disembarkation of
such a Force.

16.　　　　　On the outbreak of war the police posts
at Mandera and Moyale were withdrawn by the Civil
Authorities. This action, which has had most unfortunate
political repercussions, was done without my concurrence
or knowledge. The police posts have now been reinstituted,
and, at my request, the Governor of Kenya has placed the
police in the Northern Frontier District under my
operational command. I have prepared, with the agreement
of the Commissioner of Police and the Commissioner of the
Northern Frontier District, a plan for the action of these
police/

14.

/police in the event of war.   There will be no further withdrawal. but I have recommended to the Kenya Government that the existing police post at Mandera, the tactical situation of which is most unsound, should be moved forthwith to a position some 50 miles to the westwards

17.   Political Liaison Staff.

In view of the number of territories from which the formations and units comprising my Force are drawn, and the number of governments with which it would be necessary to communicate, (6 Governments in all exclusive of Southern Rhodesia and the West African Territories) it was decided, before the war, that a Chief Political Liaison Officer, assisted by a Political Officer from each of the territories concerned, (exclusive of Zanzibar), should be attached to my staff. The officer selected as Chief Political Liaison Officer was Sir Donald Mackenzie Kennedy, K.C.M.G., who is Governor of Nyasaland. I find it impossible to describe the assistance which I have received from the Chief Political /Liaison Officer, and I desire to place on record my sincere appreciation and thanks for the invaluable help which I have received from Sir Donald Mackenzie Kennedy and his staff. It would have been almost impossible to carry on the administration of the Force, and the general control of Military affairs throughout this vast area, without their assistance.

18.   Administrative Services.

Lieut, Colonel E. S. D. Martin, D.S,O. M.C., my A.A. & Q.M.G. arrived in Kenya on 1st September, and has been faced with almost insuperable difficulties ever since. Except for himself there is no trained/

15

/trained staff officer in either the A. or Q. branches
with the result that he has had to shoulder the large
majority of the work.

        The major problems that have confronted
my A.A. & Q.M.G. can be summarised as follows:-

(a)   No legislation had been taken in peace to
legalise the formation of the Units other than
K.A.R. enumerated in O.D.C. Memorandum 700 M.
Consequently, although all the Units were
formed on mobilisation they were illegally
constituted.

(b)   In certain of the Territories over which the
Command extends no arrangements had been made
to earmark individuals for posting to Units to
complete the War Establishment of Europeans.
This was done on mobilisation without any
pre-conceived method which resulted in many
cases in the posting to Units completely
untrained individuals. Had Italy descended
upon us before Unit Commanders had an
opportunity of gauging the Military value of
these individuals, more especially as Units
would have been operating on enormous fronts,
the result would have been disastrous.

(c)   The co-ordination of the different systems of
procedure which existed in the several
Territories over which the Command extends.

To quote two instances only:

(1)   The system of granting commissions in the
Reserve of the King's African Rifles varied,
In Territories other than Kenya, Governors
took the responsibility of granting commissions
on/

16

/on their own authority, subsequently obtaining covering approval from the Secretary of State for the Colonies. In Kenya all commissions were submitted for the approval of the Secretary of State before being granted with consequent delay in providing officers for the new units which had been raised in the Colony on mobilisation. Some 600 gentlemen have now been commissioned, and many acting promotions made.

(ii) Working out establishments and rates of pay of numerous administrative units was another heavy task. To obtain uniformity on rates of pay the Governments of six Territories had to be consulted. Consequently final agreement is still awaited in some cases, and the personnel concerned are living on provisional advances of pay.

(d) A Legal Adviser has just been appointed to my Headquarters to advise me on legal questions, which have given much anxiety in the past. This appointment is most necessary as the Defence Forces are governed by a multiplicity of Ordinances in the different Territories. In November the Law Officers of Kenya ruled that my action in raising new Units authorised by O.D.C. Memorandum 700 M. was illegal; the East African Dependencies Military Units Ordinance 1939 had therefore to be passed early in December to legalise the position.

(e) The formation of the East Africa Army Service Corps/

17

/Corps, and the East Africa Medical Corps, virtually from nothing, and without the assistance of any trained or experienced personnel other than the Heads of those Services, was a very heavy undertaking.

(f)   The shortage of boots, clothing, and the multitudinous other items required for the mobilisation of the Force necessitated the organisation of factories and shops to make good the deficiency in the shortest possible time.

(g)   In view of the fact that the peace accommodation for troops in Kenya consisted of barracks for one Battalion and the Headquarters and two Companies of another, the mobilisation and concentration of the Force necessitated the rapid construction of temporary hutted camps to accommodate it. Accommodation for Military Hospitals and for the storage of Ordnance stores and ammunition also had to be provided.

Further details concerning the difficulties which confronted my "A" Branch of the Staff are given in Appendix "L".

The manner in which Lieut. Colonel E.S.D. Martin, D.S.O., M.C., faced all these problems and gradually achieved order out of chaos, is deserving of great praise.

19. <u>Ordnance Organisation</u>.

My Assistant Director of Ordnance Services did not arrive in Kenya till 8th September. He found that the peace time system by which each unit was self-contained/

/self-contained with its own "Q" stores could not be continued in war, and accordingly set about a re-organis-ation of the military store system under central control, which will result in more equitable provision and better storage.

Staff difficulties had first to be overcome, as the only personnel available with any knowledge of store work were the Northern Brigade K.A.R. "Q" Staff, who formed a small nucleus, around which the Ordnance Staff has been built. The difficulty of working with untrained personnel was enhanced by the complete lack of copies of regulations.

Nairobi was selected as the Chief Ordnance centre in preference to the base port of Mombasa, and railhead was formed at Nanyuki. No existing military buildings were adequate as central Stores depots, but the Kenya Government and the Kenya and Uganda Railways were most helpful in providing these, either by renting existing structures, or building new ones.

Reserve stocks of military stores in the East African Territories were virtually NIL at the outbreak of war. Orders which had been placed months before with the Crown Agents had not even been ordered by them, and only now, after four months, have the first small quantities of these been delivered. Except for a few rifles and one small consignment of Bren guns, which had been on order for years, no revolvers, binoculars, compasses, web equipment, respirators or anti-gas stores have been received yet, nor any Army Forms or Training Regulations. Considerable quantities of shirts, shorts etc., have arrived; these are among the few articles which/

19

/which can be easily obtained locally.

I wish to record my appreciation
of the work that has been done on behalf of the East
Africa Force by the Kenya and Uganda Railways in their
large and well equipped workshop at Nairobi. Every
assistance in their power, and absolute priority, has been
given to our work at all time. The trial mortar made
by them proved a great success, and is not inferior to
the British product; in accuracy it is particularly
noteworthy. Approval has now been given for the
K.U.R. & H. workshop to manufacture sufficient mortars
to equip my whole Force. The South African Government
have offered me a supply of mortar sights, which is the
only component which cannot be made here, but I have not
as yet received authority to accept them.

I have had resource to local purchase
of those supplies which can be obtained in the
Territories, and in this connection the Local Tender
Boards, through whom the purchases are made, have been
of great assistance.

Further detail of Ordnance activity
is given in Appendix "M".

20. Pay.

My Command Paymaster arrived in Kenya
on 1st September, 1939.

The fixing of the rates of pay for
officers has been a most difficult matter, complicated
by a variety of conflicting considerations. My
recommendation that all officers (other than the few
Imperial Officers at Headquarters) should be paid at
African Colonial rates, was at first rejected, and
Regular/

20.

/Regular Army Reserve of Officers were placed on British rates of pay and allowances. Inequalities of these Rates compared with those of locally commissioned officers serving in the same units, and the difficulties of control and administration of their pay and allowances owing to Local Paymasters not having the necessary British Regulations, difficulties of communications and of obtaining particulars of service etc., were represented by me in numerous telegrams to the Colonial and War Offices, until on 21st November the War Office agreed to the R.A.R.O. being given African Colonial Forces rates of pay.

The new African Colonial Forces rates of pay, drawn up in peace time, included a qualifying service element; this gave rise to great difficulties in endeavouring to assess the rates of pay of the many officers called up here, and given acting rank, who have no qualifying service element. Further the officers and British N.C.O.'s of the African Colonial Forces, serving on 14th September are allowed to exercise an option to remain on the existing rates or go on to the new scales of pay; this option is still in course of being exercised, due to decisions being needed on various considerations which have been submitted by those concerned particularly K.A.R. Reserve Officers.

There is no doubt that for times of war the African Colonial Forces rates of pay are unnecessarily high. The rates were decided on in times of peace to induce officers of the British Army to serve with the African Colonial Forces. When war broke out we had no alternative but to adopt the rates which officers in the Colonies/

21

/Colonies, including those who had joined the Reserve
of the respective Africa Colonial Forces, had been led
to expect. It would have been advisable, if it had
been foreseen, to qualify the rates issuable in peace with
a statement to the effect that they would be reduced by
£100 in time of war.

Pay rates have had to be fixed for Civilian
personnel, and co-ordinated with local conditions in the
different Territories. Another matter to be adjusted was
in respect of Southern Rhodesian personnel transferred to
Units in other Territories, who were paid on a lower scale
of pay than the African Colonial Forces.

The question of the Common Charges Account,
to which war expenditure in all the Territories is charged,
has given rise to much correspondence and diversity of
opinion; and there will inevitably be disagreement when
the final allocation of expenditure is called for. In
view of the unworkable nature of the present system, a new
scheme has been agreed to, whereby all charges will be
accepted by the War Office, and annual contributions made
by the Colonies of a sum equivalent to the 1939 Military
estimates plus 25 per cent.

The East African Pay Corps has been formed
and will take charge of all Military expenditure in East
Africa from 1st January, 1940. A Military Audit Staff to
audit all military expenditure is being constituted.

Further detail is given in Appendix "N".

21. Medical.

My Assistant Director of Medical Services
arrived on 1st September, 1939. The formation of the
medical units in the East African Territories on the
outbreak/

/outbreak of war, carried out in accordance with the pre-war arrangements, disorganised the Civil Medical Administration considerably by the calling up of Government Officers, Sanitary Inspectors, and trained African personnel. When the effect of this began to be felt, requests were made for the release of essential personnel. These have been met as far as possible on condition that the personnel would be again available in an emergency. My situation with regard to medical officers is far from satisfactory.

In spite of the allotment of £15,000 by the Governments of Kenya, Uganda and Tanganyika prior to the war for the purchase of a reserve of essential drugs and dressings, there was a grave shortage of Medical Stores. The Kenya Government, however, was able to provide a bulk issue of the supplies to tide over the period until large consignments, now on order from England, arrive early in 1940.

Further detail of the medical situation is given in Appendix "O".

22.   I have referred in the course of this despatch to certain of the difficulties which I have encountered in the organisation and concentration of the Force and in implementing of the Defence Plan. I have not referred to these difficulties in any spirit of criticism, but in the hope that they may assist in presenting a complete picture of the present military situation in this area and that they may also be of some assistance when the post war military organisation in East Africa is under consideration.

23.   Shortages in weapons and military equipment generally, which, although mitigated to some extent by the/

23.

/the receipt of certain stocks since the outbreak of
war, and measures such as the local manufacture
are still causing me the greatest anxiety. These
shortages were caused partly by the financial depression
which struck these territories so heavily in the years
before the war, and partly by the inevitable delays which
the rearmament programme throughout the Empire imposed
upon the provision of military equipment and material for
these territories. A further contributory cause was the
delay imposed on our post war preparations by the
consultations which attended and followed the Norman-Newall
Report on the substitution of the greater part of the land
forces in East Africa by aircraft.

24.　　　　Since my assumption of the Command of this
Force I have been much impressed by the care with which the
plans for the organisation and concentration of the Force
were drawn up by my predecessor as Inspector General, Major
General, (now Lieut.General) G.J. Giffard, C.B., D.S.O.
Although there was insufficient time before the outbreak of
war for General Giffard's plans and arrangements to be
implemented in their entirety, a very great deal was
accomplished as a result of his labours. Without his
preliminary planning my task would have been infinitely
more difficult, and it is doubtful whether any organised
force for the defence of East Africa could have been
concentrated without a delay of many months.

25.　　　　I desire to take this opportunity of
expressing my appreciation of the assistance which has been
rendered to me by the Government of Southern Rhodesia from
the outbreak of the war. Not only has this Government
implemented/

24.

/implemented all the commitments undertaken by them prior
to the war, but on every occasion when I have been in
difficulties they have invariably met my requests for
assistance, even at considerable inconvenience to themselves.

26.   The Director General of Operations, Union
of South Africa, Colonel P. de Waal, visited my Headquarters
from the 20th to 29th November. As a result of this visit
I received the most detailed information regarding the
defence organisation and plans in the Union. This has been
communicated to the War Office. I also supplied Colonel
de Waal with full information regarding the military
situation in this area.

On the 23rd December a further reconnaissance
party from Defence Headquarters, Pretoria arrived at my
Headquarters. The task of these officers was to carry out
a preliminary reconnaissance of the route from South Africa
to Kenya, with a view to the possibility of utilising it
for the transportation, in an emergency, of South African
troops to Kenya. A further and more detailed reconnaissance
of this route is about to be undertaken by South Africa
Defence Headquarters.

27.   I cannot close this despatch without placing
on record my deep appreciation of the assistance I have
always received from Their Excellencies the Governors and.
the Governments of all Territories over which my Command
extends viz:-

Air Chief Marshall Sir Robert Brooke-Popham, K.C.V.O., K.C.B.,
D.S.O. and latterly Mr Walter Harragin, K.C., and the Governor
of Kenya.

25

Sir Mark Young, K.C.M.G. and the Government,   Tanganyika.
Sir Philip Mitchell , K.C.M.G. and the Government, Uganda.
Mr John Maybin, K.C.M.G. and the Government,   N. Rhodesia.
Mr. K. L. Hall, C.M.G. and the Government,   Nyasaland.
Mr. J. H. Hall, C.M.G. and the Government,   Zanzibar.

28.   Finally I wish to bring to your notice
the names of the undermentioned officers who, in the
difficult circumstances I have referred to in the preceding
paragraphs, have worked untiringly to place the East Africa
Force on an efficient basis.

Sir Donald Mackenzie Kennedy, K.C.M.G., Chief Political
                              Liaison Officer.
Mr. R,A.J. Maguire, Secretary to the Chief Political
                              Liaison Officer,
Lieutenant Colonel E.S.D. Martin, D.S.O., M.C. - A.A.G. & Q.M.G.
Brevet Lieutenant Colonel W.H.A. Bishop   - G.S.O.1.
Brevet Colonel C. P. Herbert, M.C.   - Command Paymaster and
                              Financial Adviser.
Brigadier C.C. Fowkes, C.B.E., MC. - Commander 2nd E.A.
                              Infantry Brigade.
Brigadier D. M. Barchard,   - Commander 1st E.A.
                              Infantry Brigade,
Brigadier G. L. Easton, M.C.   - Commander, Lines of
                              Communication Area,
Lieutenant Colonel T.A. Dillon   - Commander, 1st Bn.
                              King's African Rifles.
Acting Lieutenant Colonel N.R.G. Tucker - Commander, 2nd Bn,
                              King's African Rifles,
Acting Lieutenant Colonel N.A. Thorp, Commander, 3rd Bn.
                              King's African Rifles.
Lieutenant Colonel W. A. Dimoline, M.C. - Commander, 1st Bn.
                              Northern Rhodesia Regt.
Acting Lieutenant Colonel T.M. Brick, O.B.E. -E.A.A.S.C.
Lieutenant Colonel J.W. Gaisford,   A.D.O.S.
Lieutenant Colonel P.R. Mundy, D.S.O., O.B.E., M.C, -
                              Commander, 4th Bn.
                              King's African Rifles.

Lieutenant/

26.

Lieutenant Colonel H.A. Case, C.M.G., C.B.E., D.S.O.,
                          Commander, 2nd Echelon.
Hon. Brigadier General A.C. Lewin, C.B., C.M.G., D.S.O., A.D.C.
                          Commander, Officers
                          Training School.
Lieutenant Colonel T.B. Butt,   Chief Instructor,
                          Officers Training School.

I have the honour to be,
Sir,
Your obedient servant,

,

[Sgd Dickinson]
Major General.
General Officer Commanding.
EAST AFRICA FORCE.

APPENDICES ATTACHED

A.   Summary of events in East Africa, as
          Recorded in the War Diary, Headquarters,
          E.A. Force.

B.   Supply and Transport.

C.   Intelligence.

D.   Survey and Maps.

E.   Royal Engineers.

F.   Signal Communications.

G.   Map.

H.   Location Statement.

J.   Air Forces in East Africa.

L.   "A" Branch Difficulties.

M.   Ordnance.

N.   Pay, Services and Financial Control.

O.   Medical Situation.

- - - -

[Lettering is as per original]

DIARY OF EVENTS IN EAST AFRICA
AS RECORDED IN THE WAR DIARY HEADQUARTERS, E.A.FORCE,

1.   On receipt of a telegram from the Secretary of State on
August 25th ordering the mobilization of the African Colonial
Forces, all units were ordered, on August 26th, to mobilize
at their peace stations.

On August 28th Classes 1 and 2 of the Kenya Defence
Force were called up; and on the following day posts and
patrols furnished by this unit were instructed to take up
positions of readiness on the Kenya-Tanganyika border.

On August 29th the Southern Rhodesia Air Unit, (now
designated No.1 Squadron, Southern Rhodesia Air Force),
arrived in Nairobi with 9 aircraft, to replace No. 223 Bomber
Squadron, R.A.F. which had proceeded to Middle East in
accordance with the War plan.

On August 31st Headquarters, East Africa Force was
established at Kenton College, near Nairobi.

On September 1st the Precautionary Stage in the Defence
Scheme came into operation and Air Restrictions wore imposed.

On September 3rd the "War with Germany" telegram was
despatched to all units and formations at 13.30 hours.

2.   Issue of Operation Instructions by Headquarters, E.A.Force.
September 1st 1939. Operation Instruction No. 1.

This instruction laid down the dispositions and tasks of
all units in the Force, (a), during the "stand-by period["], and
(b), during the Precautionary Period. Briefly, these
dispositions wore designed to hold the line of the TANA and
UASO NYIRO rivers, and to watch the approaches towards
GARTSSA and along the Coastal Belt. The R.A.F. was assigned
the task of reconnoitring the main approaches from Italian East
Africa. Administrative, Medical and Intercommunication
instructions were also included.

2

<u>September 2nd 1939</u>, Operation Instruction No. 2.
4 K.A.R. (less 3 Coys.) to be held in readiness as a
striking force to move out at short notice to protect the
Kenya-Uganda railway against possible raids by German
nationals from Tanganyika. 3rd K.A.R. warned to hold a
detachment in readiness to protect the railway between
Nairobi and Voi (exclusive).

<u>September 2nd 1939</u>. Operation Instruction No. 3.

Orders for action to be taken by Uganda Police Service
Coy. at LOKITAUNG (TURKANA) in the event of their having
to withdraw; and for demolitions on the road on the NEPAU
pass and SUK escarpment.

<u>September 3rd 1939</u>. Operation Instruction No. 4.

4 K.A.R. (less 3 Coys) to move to Mackinnon Road Station
K.U. Railway and to occupy water-holes between the
Tanganyika border and the railway in order to intercept
German nationals from Tanganyika in any attempt to raid
the railway line.

<u>September 8th 1939</u>. Operation Instruction No. 5.

To Officer Commanding, 5th K.A.R. One rifle company to
be detailed to accompany Commissioner, N.F.D. on his re-
occupation of the Civil Post at MOYALE.

<u>September 9th 1939</u>. Operation Instruction No. 6.

To Commander Local Forces. Instructions to re-open the
Tanganyika Frontier and to withdraw guards on vital points,
except wireless installations and petrol dumps.

<u>September 10th 1939</u>. The 22nd Mountain Battery, R.A. arrived
at Mombasa from India, and proceeded by rail to camp in
the vicinity of Nairobi.

<u>September 17th 1939</u>. Operation Instruction No. 7.

This instruction contained amendments to Operation

3

Instructions 1 and 2. The East bank of the Tana River
through BURA to GARISSA, thence LORIAN Swamp –
HABASWEIN –
MERTI – ARCHER'S POST to be the main defended line. The
wells at WAJIR and MARSABIT to be denied to the enemy.

4th K.A.R. to check any advance along the coastal route.
5th K.A.R., LORIAN Swamp to MERTI, (both inclusive), and
to hold the wells at WAJIRD.

1st K.A.R. ARCHER'S POST – ISIOLO; one Company to defend
the wells at MARSABIT. Reserves at KITUI and NANYUKI.
Reconnaissance of above positions, and wiring of main line
and WAJIR and MARSABIT to be carried out forthwith. This
Instruction also included Signal Instruction No. 1 giving
arrangements for intercommunication, and administrative
orders regarding supplies of rations and ammunition.

At the same time orders were issued to the Southern
Rhodesia Air Unit to be prepared to furnish information in
the event of war regarding every movement along the coastal
route and from the direction of MOYALE.

September 25th 1939. Operation Instruction No. 8.

Notifying certain preliminary moves of formations and
units from L. of C. area to Nairobi in order to facilitate
the adoption of the war plan.

2nd October 1939. Operation Instruction No. 9.
The preliminary moves as detailed in Operation
Instruction No. 8 to be carried out. The line to be denied
to the enemy, in the event of war with Italy, during the
wet season (Oct.15th /Dec. 15th) was amended as follows:-
Garsen, Bura – Garissa – Mana – Isiolo – Archer's Post.
The Commandcr at Marsabit a delaying action along
the road Moyale – Turbi – Marsabit – Archer's Post.

Roads Isiolo – for 25 miles towards Garba Tulla and.
Isiolo – Archer's Bridge to be made all-weather.

The existing Scout Platoon to reorganize in Nairobi
as a Reconnaissance Squadron,

4

29th October 1939, Operation Instruction No. 10.
Modified instructions regarding the defence of the N.F.D.
In the event of war with Italy, 22nd Mountain Battery and
the 1st E.A. Light Battery move to Nanyuki.
Administrative: Rations for 3 months to be dumped as
follows:-
At MOYALE – for 1 Battalion.
At WAJIR – for 1 Battalion
At MURSABIT – for 1 Company

3. Movements of Troops
During the period under review the following
important movements have taken place:-
September 10th Civil Police Posts at MOYALE and MANDERA,
which had been evacuated on the outbreak of war with
Germany by order of the Civil authorities, were re-occupied
without incident on Sept. 14th and 18th respectively.
October 12th Headquarters 2nd E.A. Infantry Brigade,
Signal Section, and 6th K.A.R. arrived at NANYUKI from
L. of C. area. 1st K.A.R. moved to JINJA, but was later
moved into the 2nd E.A. Infantry Brigade area at Nanyuki.
The 1st Bn. Kenya Regiment (T.A.) arrived at Kampala
from Nairobi on October 8th.
October 28th 2nd K.A.R. arrived in Nairobi from Moshi
and Iringa, and was transferred from 2nd to 1st E.A.
Infantry Brigade from that date.
October 25th. 1 Company Northern Rhodesia Regiment
arrived at Moshi and 1 Company at Iringa (from Lusaka).

4. Formation of New Units.
Since the outbreak of war, the following new units have
been formed in East Africa:-
1st E.A. Light Battery.
1st Field Survey Coy & E.A. Engineers.

5

1st Field Company, E.A. Engineers.
E.A. Reconnaissance Squadron.
1st Battalion E.A. Pioneer.
2nd Battalion E.A. Pioneer.
7th Battalion K A.R. (T.A.)
2/6th Battalion K.A.R.
2nd Battalion Northern Rhodesia Regiment.
East Africa Army Service Corps.
East Africa Medical Corps.
East Africa Pay Corps   }
Military Audit Unit   }
1st Donkey Coy. E. Africa Pack Transport Corps.

5   Training.

Owing to the neutral attitude adopted by Italy,
and the consequent situation, intensive training was
ordered for all units in the E.A. Force. This also
included Medical and Transport Units, whose expansion.
to war strength as laid down in O.D.C. 700 M. has
proceeded actively.

A School of Instruction for Officers was
established at Nakuru on October 24th; a first
course for 79 students from the Kenya Regiment and. K.A.R.
commencing on that date; the number of students
being later increased to 120. On the second course.
commencing on February 8th, 150 students will be
accommodated. On the conclusion of this course the
school will, in accordance with order received from
the War Office, be disbanded.

SUPPLY AND TRANSPORT

1 ORGANIZATION'

(a)   My A.D.S. & T. arrived on the 1st September and found himself faced with an unfamiliar organization and varied system of administration spread over the five territories.

To meet such a situation there was no staff available and he was forced to organize his office with an improvised staff. Owing to the necessary expansion of the East African Army Service Corps (sec Table "A") with a nucleus of only four officers, it was not possible for him to call in any of these to assist him. Working practically single handed he had to assume full responsibility of the administration of the supply and transport services in East Africa. He soon decided that he must have subordinate officers on the supply and transport side of his staff but it was not possible to find suitable officers until the end of October. No establishment existed for them on this Headquarters and it was found necessary to place them on the establishment of the Headquarters of Lines of Communication and attach them here. Should active operations take place and the Lines of Communication be called upon to function as such, these officers would have to be restored to their Headquarters and an increase demanded to this establishment.

(b)   DRIVER PERSONNEL

The rates of pay laid down for native drivers in peace time were not sufficient to draw recruits and the procedure of having new rates of pay approved by all Governments concerned caused long delay. These have now been agreed to and wired to the War Office for covering approval. Owing to this delay the driver position is far from satisfactory and may take at least three to four months to bring the required

2

number to an efficient standard of driving. Owing to the rapid expansion it has been found difficult to find suitable men to promote to non-commissioned rank and the standard of discipline has suffered accordingly. It has now been discovered that the East African Army Service Corps has not been legally constituted. Consequently all ranks will have to be re-attested under the new Ordinance and it is likely that many will prefer to take their discharge. This again has put back the training and efficiency of the drivers by several months.

(c) <u>WORKSHOP PERSONNEL</u>

It is not easy to find suitable workshop personnel in East Africa. Apprenticed natives are few and the average mechanic is of a very low standard. Indian artificers, apart from carpenters and blacksmiths, are of a similar low standard. In peace time technical work is normally done by white labour and even this type of mechanic is not always articled.

From the above it will be realised that suitable personnel for mobile and heavy workshops will take considerable time to have suitably trained.

(d) <u>ESTABLISHMENTS</u>.

The existing Establishments allow for no decentralization within the East African Army Service Corps. It was found impossible for the Commanding Officer to control the units formed in each territory according to O.D.C. 700M. It has therefore been necessary to appoint an Officer Commanding East African Army Service Corps base units in Nairobi and Commanding Officer East African Army Service Corps in each territory. Had such organization been arranged in peace time my A.D.S. & T. could have received information of how the expansion was progressing.

3

Until such organization was instituted it was almost
impossible for the Supply and Transport Directorate to
know of the progress being made. Owing to the shortage
of staff and clerical personnel, requisitioning of
vehicles, purchasing of chassis, manufacture of bodies,
registration and issue of vehicles to units, the formation
of the East African Army Service Corps is by no means
near completion,

2. SUPPLIES
    (a) CHANGE OF MOBILIZATION
        Before the war rationing of the troops was done by
    contract through the Central Tender Board of each territory
    concerned. The King's African Rifles Transport Corps
    undertook the delivery but had no supply section attached
    to it. On mobilization this system ceased and the East
    African Army Service Corps commenced to function as a
    supply unit.

    (b) PERSONNEL
    On mobilization personnel chosen from the Kenya
    Defence Force were allotted to the various duties at the
    Main and Field Supply Depots. With the exception of a few
    of the officers who served in the late war, this personnel
    had received no previous training in supply duties. It
    can be readily realized that general confusion set in.
    In spite of the initial difficulties the active assistance
    of the Regular Officers and B.N.C.O.'s gradually solved
    the situation. Unavoidably certain losses of rations
    occurred in the Northern Frontier District, but these
    losses were less than might have been expected owing to the
    lack of experience of the supply personnel.

    (c) RATIONS
        The Kenya Farmers Association had boon appointed
    buying agents by the Government for all food stuff

4

required in Kenya. On mobilization rations were handed over by this organization to the Main Supply Depot. This system has worked well and the quality of rations supplied has generally been good.

In Uganda and Tanganyika the food controller supplied the rations but since the increase in troops they have found difficulty in meeting full requirements. In Uganda a Field Supply Depot has now been established and in Tanganyika the formation of one is taking place.

Prior to the war no organization of a military supply system existed. If it had not been for the assistance of the local supply boards the system would have broken down.

(d) <u>PETROL</u>

The only bulk tanks in the country are at Mombasa and owing to the danger of this town from air attack, the Government just prior to the War stored one and a quarter million gallons in tins, mostly uncased, over Kenya and Uganda. The storage of this petrol was arranged hurriedly and not according to military regulations, with the result that a considerable loss has been incurred through leakage, Buildings, many miles from an A.S.C. Unit, were packed to the roof so that the bottom four-gallon tins (the only containers available) were in most cases "concertina-ed". Stocks also were of such a size that it was impossible to check their contents or to detect undue wastage. The Governments concerned contend that they had not the staff or the facilities for supervising this storage and, as it was carried out for military requirements, that the Army must assume responsibility. It has therefore been necessary to build sheds and to restack in accordance with regulations. There is a danger, however, that the stocks are so great and the consumption, in the absence of active operations, so small, that "gumming" may set in before the

5

supply can be used up. Owing to the fact that
hostilities have not broken out, certain stocks are
being handed back to the oil companies to avoid leakage
and the danger of gumming. As a precaution against
the latter danger a tin from each store is being sent
monthly for analysis.

Considerable wastage has occurred for the reason
stated above and through transporting petrol in encased
four gallon tins over the rough roads. To minimize the
latter I have arranged for a board of civilian experts
to consider the best means of carriage and prevention
of leakage.

3. TRANSPORT
   (a) Requisitioning of Vehicles.

The system of requisitioning did not prove satisfactory. Instead of being registered, inspected and
tested in peace time, vehicles were brought in from all
over the country and valued by an Impressment Board to
which no military officers had been appointed. In
Nairobi many vehicles were rejected by an officer at
the place of impressment, but at outlying stations this
was impossible, with the result that many unserviceable
vehicles were taken over. Besides, the majority of
vehicles were without tools, spare wheel, or equipment,
and the tyres were considerably worn. It is understood
that it is not unusual for vehicles to be without proper
equipment, but the result is that some sixty six thousand
pounds (this figure is likely to be considerably
increased before the Force is completed) have been, up to
the present, spent on equipping such vehicles (exclusive
of chains) and a further considerable sum on making them
fit for the road. It is agreed that there was no
alternative but to accept most of the vehicles offered at

the beginning of September as they were necessary for the immediate formation of the units, should Italy have come into the war, but a good number have had to be written off since as unrepairable. Undoubtedly, the lack of pre-war organization caused extra expense.

The life of vehicles in this country, over bad roads and with indifferent drivers, is short, and if it had been known that time was available it would certainly have been more economical to have purchased new vehicles. As it was, and under the circumstances prevailing, over 800 new vehicles had to be bought immediately, to make good deficiencies in rejected vehicles and to complete the new units approved by W.O. to their authorised establishment at a cost of over £500,000 inclusive of insurance, freight and locally manufactured bodies.

Transport requisitioned by local authorities (some 1200) cost approximately £250,000.

(b) Repairs

The Financial Secretary of Kenya advised that the system of repairs would be more economically carried out in the local garages under military supervision. The advantages of this system being a saving of rent, lighting, wages, etc., the possibility of returning to normal at short notice, and overcoming the difficulty of recruiting suitable artificers. Owing to the lack of control this system has not proved successful and it has now been decided to open a heavy repair shop.

(c) Motor Transport Stores,=

The same policy as for "Repairs" was recommended for M.M.T. Stores Depot. It is considered, however, that a large part of what we are now spending could be saved by holding stocks purchased free of import duty. Accommodation is being sought and stores demanded. It is

7

considered that special military terms should be given by the railway and that Government stores should be admitted free of duty. This question is being taken up.

TABLE A

	PERSONNEL									VEHICLES							
	European			Africans				Non-Combatants									
	Officers	W & NCOs	TOTAL	Sgt Majors	Sergeants	Rank & File	TOTAL	Asians	Africans	Lorries	M/Cycles	Bicycles	Motorcars	W/Lorry	B/Lorry	Spares Lorry	M/Ambulance
(i) Establishment of T.C., K.A.R. on outbreak of hostilities																	
Regular	4	4	8	1	4	19	24	9	81	58	2	2	-	-	-	-	-
Reserves	21		21			7	7		25								
Supplementary Reserves									166								
TOTAL	25	4	29	1	4	26	31	9	272	58	2	2	-	-	-	-	-
(ii) Initial requirements for the 1st E.A. & 1st W.A. Bdes	86	247	333	1	17	378	396	159	2049	1195	198	91	155	23	22	20	62
(iii) Revised requirements as on 12.12.1939	146	454	600	9	65	677	751	316	4298	2938	311	56	442	41	31	31	84
(iv) Strength as on 27.11.1939	91	342	415	1	8	241	260	218	2143	1314	108	23	398	4	4	2	76

APPENDIX "C"

INTELLIGENCE

Previous to the outbreak of war no arrangements had been made for the creation of an Intelligence Organisation in East Africa.

Accordingly an entirely new organisation had to be built up speedily for the collection of information in the frontier districts. A number of white hunters and other men with knowledge of the country were enrolled, and stationed in the N.F.D. at Moyale, Wajir, Marsabit, Mandera and Garissa. This organisation was put under Captain J.W.L. Llewellin, an ex-administrative officer with a long experience of the N.F.D. and knowledge of the Somalis. At a later date another intelligence agent was stationed at Lamu. These agents working in pairs are responsible for the collection of intelligence, particularly from over the border, in the extensive districts covered by their posts. They patrol the roads and cover the border in their districts, getting information from tribesmen, police and travellers and keeping Headquarters informed of the state of the roads, water supplies, native opinion etc. In all this they work in the closest touch with the Administration and Police officials of the district. The work in the arid desert country which is the Northern Frontier District of Kenya, is extremely arduous; the appalling roads do much damage to the transport, lack of water, heat and dust make the living conditions severe. These agents have stuck to their work and sent in much useful information to Headquarters.

IEA Intelligence

The organisation outlined above has proved most useful in obtaining information regarding frontier affairs

particularly/

2

particularly the strengths and details of Italian banda dispositions and reports of shifta activity across the border. But it is not adequate to obtain accurate and detailed information of Italian troop dispositions and activities further inland. The absolute ban on the employment of paid agents to cross the border imposed. to avoid any chance of antagonising Italy, has made it most difficult to get this type of intelligence.

Ciphers and Codes.

A great deal of work was entailed at the beginning of the war in the issuing and taking into immediate use throughout the Force of the various ciphers and code names which were necessary. This was satisfactorily achieved, though a great strain was put on the cipher personnel at first, when the new staff were learning their work, and cipher telegrams were passing in and out at a high rate. A cipher officer (2/Lt. Mullin) and a sergeant arrived out from England on the 9th Sept. and took over the control of ciphers and code names throughout the Force.

Censorship.

This was instituted throughout the East African territories at the outbreak of war, and was undertaken by the civil authorities.

Close touch has been maintained with the civil Censorship, and interesting information is received from time to time as a result of their scrutiny of correspondence.

Propaganda.

The Information Committee under civil direction is responsible for all propaganda by wireless and the press. Contact is maintained by my staff with the Ministry to ensure that propaganda favourable to the military is encouraged, and adverse criticism counteracted.

APPENDIX "D"

SURVEY AND MAPS

(i) <u>1st Field Survey Company, East African Engineers.</u>

Prior to the outbreak of war, the question of the formation of survey units in the African colonial territories was under consideration with the Colonial Office. Tanganyika Territory Survey Department had prepared a comprehensive scheme during 1939, and when the order was received they were able rapidly to mobilize at Dar-es-Salaam. Within a few days the Headquarters, one Field Topographical Section, and a Map Production Section of a Field Survey Company, under Major Rowe, Director of Surveys, T.T., were formed and undergoing military training.

A second Field Topographical Section was formed later at Nairobi largely from personnel of the Kenya and Uganda Survey Departments.

No.1 Field Topo. Section moved up to Nairobi on 16/9/39 and proceeded to the Northern Frontier District, where they started on the mapping of this vast area, of which maps were urgently required for military purposes, as it might be expected that should Italy enter the war against us this night well be the scene of operations.

No.2 Section followed them into the field on 14/11/39.

The procedure adopted was to undertake a series of road traverses with astronomical control, putting in as much detail as possible in the course thereof. It is intended to fill in detail by aerial photography between these roads and in certain areas difficult to survey by ground methods, and which are of Military importance. A map on a scale of 1:250,000 will be produced from these. In certain areas of tactical importance e.g. around vital stations and river

crossings/

2,

crossings it is intended to produce 1:50,000 maps for military use. In this way the Northern Frontier District and the Tana River valley should shortly be adequately surveyed and mapped.

A third Field Topographical Section, to act as a Reserve and training Section, is being formed in Nairobi.

Southern Rhodesia offered to raise a Field Survey Company and to put it at my disposal for use in Kenya, but to date War Office permission to accept the offer has not yet been received.

(ii) <u>Map Reproduction.</u>

The Map Production Section of the 1st Field Survey Coy. E.A.E. at Dar-es-Salaam undertook and carried out the reproduction of an Italian map of Italian East Africa, scale 1:1,000,000, which had come into the possession of the Intelligence Officer, Northern Brigade K.A.R. just prior to hostilities. The map, in a series of 15 sheets, was reproduced in four colours at an average rate of under 20 days per sheet for 100 copies, including photography, taking off and inking up of blue pulls, printing names, and the final printing in four colours (not however layered like the original). Half of the copies were given a military grid. These excellent results wore obtained by dint of very hard work, the staff working day and night in 8 hour shifts.

Other smaller jobs, such as reproduction of a map of the Eastern Front, camp sites, diagrams for training manuals etc. have boon undertaken. A training map of Isiolo is in hand for use in manoeuvres in the New Year. The field work of the topographical sections is now coming in, and the first provisional sheets in the N.F.D. have been brought out.

/3

3

(iii) <u>Map Supplies.</u>

Steps had been taken during 1938-39 to ensure
that adequate supplies of such maps of East Africa as
existed should be available in the territories in the event
of war. Supplies in bulk of G.S.G.S. and Ordnance Survey
maps had been on order from England, but delays in carrying
out the orders resulted in only one half of the maps
arriving in East Africa by the outbreak of War. A further
consignment arrived after about one month, and the final
cases in November.

ROYAL ENGINEERS.

1.   My Commander Royal Engineers was appointed to Force Headquarters on September 26th. Up to this date all Military work had been carried out under the A.A.Q.M.G. by the P.W.D., Kenya and Uganda Railways & Harbours, Municipalities and District Councils. The P.W.D. in addition to works ordered by Force Headquarters were hard put to carry out other Military works which had been authorised by the Civil Government prior to or on the outbreak of War of which little or nothing was known at Force Headquarters. This meant that at the very time when pre-organised supervision and co-ordination of Engineer Services was most urgently required, both in the forward areas and Lines of Communication, it was to all intents and purposes non-existent. Consequently delays and confusion in the execution of the large number of Engineer Services were inevitable.

2.   In addition to the normal works services there were major field works and problems concerned with the operations side, comprising roads, water supplies, demolition etc, that had to be reconnoitred, co-ordinated and got under way. This was made increasingly difficult by the absence of Engineer troops of any description,

3.   The problem as to how best to get an adequate and efficient organisation going, even assuming it would be authorised, was still further complicated by the/–

2

/the fact that as hostilities had not broken out, it was necessary to curtail expenditure as far as possible, bearing in mind that all military works had to be carried out under conditions which were neither those of Peace nor War. It was also apparent that if even the most elementary control of expenditure was to be maintained, works adequately supervised and expeditiously executed, a very considerable engineering staff would be essential for Kenya Colony apart from the other four Territories.

4.   Considerable delay was experienced in getting the position of C.R.E. authorised. In the meantime it was realised that certain reconnaissances of strategic roads both in the Northern Frontier District and elsewhere called for immediate action for which an Officer was duly appointed. The post of A.C.R.E. to take charge of Works Service was imperative together with a Works Officer to assist in the control and execution of similar works in Mombasa and the Coastal Area.

5.   As has been previously stated, prior to the establishment of the C.R.E. branch at Force Head-quarters, all military works had been executed by the various Civil Departments, and financial control and supervision on behalf of the Military was not possible. To check and curtail any unwarranted expenditure and to standardise the works, the C.R.E. branch now holds a strict watching brief over all Military Works and the following procedure is adopted:-

> (a) All requisitions for Works, other than those
> covered by G.R.O. No. 152, must be made to
> Force Headquarters.
> (b) The D.A.Q.M.G. then refers the subject,
> with his recommendations, to the C.R.E.

3

     (c) The C.R.E. checks the specifications and estimates, (or prepares them) inspects the site etc., and submits his recommendations to C.P. through "Q".

     (d) Final financial authority for the work to proceed, or otherwise, is then obtained from the C.P.

     (e) When the work is authorised to proceed, the Department responsible for its execution is advised and during the construction it is inspected by the C.R.E. branch.

     Followed by a final inspection when the work is completed.

6.   Schedule "B" attached is a summary of Works that have been supervised by the C.R.E. to date. Before the establishment of the C.R.E. branch certain works had already been completed or were in course of construction, and it was not possible to exercise control, but Schedule "B" attached will serve to show some of the economies since effected as the result of recommendations and modifications by the C.R.E. branch. It will be seen that owing to this control a saving of approximately 50% has been effected, and this "Tightening-up" of expenditure is resulting in less elaborate and more economical standards of work being prepared by the Civil Departments concerned.

7.   Every endeavour is now being made by C.R.E. branch to relieve the various Civil Departments of administrative and executive works, thereby reducing the cost of the works, as well as saving overheads covering salaries, and other allowances. The C.R.E. branch is now approaching the position of being able to prepare its own specifications/-

4

/specifications, site plans, working drawings and estimates, and control in detail of the estimates prepared by the Civil Departments.

The branch is also able to supervise to some extent, the execution of works being carried out by Civil Departments. It is proposed in the near future to establish a C.R.E. Tender Board – Tenders for Works will then be dealt with by Force Headquarters, and contracts awarded direct, thereby avoiding the delays and misunderstandings now caused by first passing all works through the P.W.D. and other Civil Departments.

It should be appreciated that in addition to the preparation, supervision and inspection of all works services, the Headquarters staff is also responsible for normal routine matters and has to deal with a large amount of correspondence each day.

8.   The P.W.D. and other Civil Departments have given most valuable assistance under adverse conditions, since, apart from the sudden changes in policy inseparable from Military operations, it has been necessary in many instances to leave them in ignorance of the exact reason for the execution or modification of certain works. It therefore follows that the more self contained and effective the C.R.E. branch becomes, the less will it be necessary to call upon the Civil Departments to perform works, the reason and necessity for which is not always clear to them.

A complete taking over from the Civil Departments of all Military works is neither desirable nor possible with the semi-Peace time establishment under which the C.R.E. branch is operating, but even with its present establishment a definite improvement in expediency and economy may safely be anticipated,

MILITARY WORKS – NAIROBI

STATEMENT OF PAYMENTS AND ESTIMATED COSTS

Name of Work	ESTIMATED FINAL COST			
	Buildings	Electric Light	Water Supply	Total
	£	£	£	£
Petrol Storage, Kahawa	1,900	-	-	1,900
Military Camp & C.C.S. (Uganda), Show Ground Kabete	9,200	550	Included	9,750
Accommodation for Royal Corps of Signals, Kabete	900	100	Included	1,000
3rd K.A.R. Lines at Jeannes School, Kabete	6,500	325	Including est. for purification 1,200	8,025
Ordnance Stores, K.A.R. Lines, Nairobi	2,950	50	Included	3,000
Details Camp, K.A.R. Lines Nairobi	2,263	-	Included	2,263
Mbagathi Camp	7,500	-	2,800	10,300
Auxiliary Accommodation B.N.C.O.'s at Ordnance stores	585	15	Included	600
Splinter-proofing Military Garages, Nairobi	1,220	-	-	1,220
Forces Headquarters & Hostel Various Additions Darkening Windows	1,750	125	-	1,875
Area Headquarters, Ditto	35	-	Sanitary work 15	50
E.A.A.S.C. Depot. V.R.D. Park	170	50	Roads etc 50	270
E.A.A.S.C. Depot. V.R.D. Accommodation generally	-	-	Sanitary arrangements 270	270
Military School of Instruction, Nakuru Show Ground	2,350	150	Est. for purification not included	2,500
TOTALS £	37,323	1,365	4,335	43,023
V.D. Accommodation, Nairobi Show Ground	Nil			Say £2,000
Bridge, Mbagathi Road				270
Minor Works			Say	200

TOTAL   £   45,493

MILITARY WORKS

NYERI AREA

			£
(a)	Ordnance Store, Nanyuki	Complete	672
(b)	Alterations to (a) To accommodate British N.C.O.'s	Complete	59
(c)	Temporary works at Nanyuki Lines	Complete	138
(d)	Additional Kitchens – Nanyuki Lines	Complete	100
(e)	Roads – Nanyuki Area – £3,200 Bitumen carpet section Allocation not received for 6 miles water-bound section		500
(f)	Roads – Northern Frontier District Construction Co. contract Work on Garbatulla section Huts, temporary staff	say £2,500 to date	

TOTAL   £3,969

- - - - -

NAIROBI AREA

		£
(a)	E.A.A.S.C. Depot Nairobi Extra water tanks and redecoration of house for Officers plus mosquito gauze for meat store and cook houses	208
(b)	Alterations of Y.M.C.A. Building for Local Forces Headquarters	120
(c)	Brigade Headquarters, match-board lining to office of Chief Paymaster and staff	80
(d)	Storage of petrol, Ruiru and Kahawa, grass cutting and alterations to store	54
(e)	Emergency Petrol Store, Garissa	167
(f)	K,A.R. Store, Nairobi Alterations as temporary G.A. Ammunition and Explosives Magazine	200

TOTAL   £   809

MOMBASA AREA

		£
(a)	Camouflaging Oil Installations Mombasa	1,000
(b)	Various works for Fortress K.D.F. Coast Rifle Co. Coast Defence Battery 4th K.A.R. (Details to be given later)	850 approx
(c)	Transport, handling charges, etc for military works	320 approx
(d)	Barbed wire fencing, Prohibited Area	1,000
(e)	Eritrean Deserters' Camp Gotani	3,000 approx
(f)	Coast Rifle Co.	2,000 approx Only est awaited

(g) E.A.A.S.C. Depot, Mariakani
   (i) Materials   365)
   (ii) Erection   500) approx.
   (iii) Dismantling   200) say   2,065
   (iv) Ordnance Store   1000)

TOTAL £10,235

- - -

ABSTRACT	£
Head Office	45,493
Mombasa Area	10,235
Nyeri Area	3,969
Nairobi Area	809
TOTAL	£60,506

The figures given are tentative only and do not include for supervision charges if Government decides to impose such.

Add for expenses in connection with Pioneer Battalions, 1st September to 11th November, £14,206 (1st September to 27th October chargeable to Common Charges Account. From 28th October to 11th November an adjustment account will be forwarded chargeable Military)

SCHEDULE "B"

	Original Estimate	Revised Estimate	Saving
1. Training School for Officers	£5,100	£2,500	£ 600
2. Mbagathi Camp additions	1,161	499	662
3. V.D. Hospital	810	600	210
4. Casualty Clearing Station Nairobi	1,750	1,050	700
5. E.A.A.S.C additional accommodation }			
6. New proposal for Accommodation }	7,000	2,500	4,500
TOTALS	£13,821	£7,149	£6,672

Saving effected approximately 50%

SIGNAL COMMUNICATIONS.

My Chief Signal Officer arrived at end of August, a few days before war was declared.

There were then no Army W/T Sets in East Africa, the few existing W/T Sets having been made in the Signal Workshop from time to time. Telephonic and telegraphic communications were inadequate, and speech over the existing lines was poor; general improvements had to be carried out. No line communications existed, or exist now between Isiolo and the 300 miles to the Northern Frontier.

No reserves of permanent line stores were available in Kenya, Tanganyika or Uganda. Cables were despatched to the War Office requesting supplies of permanent line stores and the required W/T Sets, and a small reserve of permanent line stores was obtained from South Africa.

There was no Headquarters Signal Office until the arrival of Force Headquarters Signals at the end of September, which was a great handicap during the already difficult period when Headquarters was being formed. Temporary Despatch Riders had to be engaged, and personnel were all untrained.

On enquiring into the existing Signal organisation, my Chief Signal Officer learnt that many permanent W/T Sets were spread over the Northern Frontier District. The sets and operators belonged for the most part to the Northern Brigade Signal Section, and in consequence this section could not have functioned as a brigade signal section should they have had to go on active operations.

None of the permanent Stations in the Northern Frontier District could be dispensed with and it was/-

2

/was with difficulty that the necessary W/T equipment
and reserve personnel to keep them all in being were
collected.

A new organisation had to be prepared for
Northern Area Signals and Lines of Communication Area
Signals to ensure that the two Brigade Signal Sections
were entirely separate from the permanent W/T organisation,
and in a position to accompany their Brigades in the field.

Stores for Headquarters Signals have only
just arrived; the Brigade Signal Section W/T Sets are
not yet here, but they are expected shortly.

No W/T Lorries exist in East Africa, and
special bodies have had to be built. There is a shortage
of motor bicycles, and most of those requisitioned were in
a bad condition, and not fit for active service conditions.

The present situation with regard to the
signal organisation in this Command is shown in detail in
the attached table.

SIGNAL ORGANISATION IN EAST AFRICA FORCE

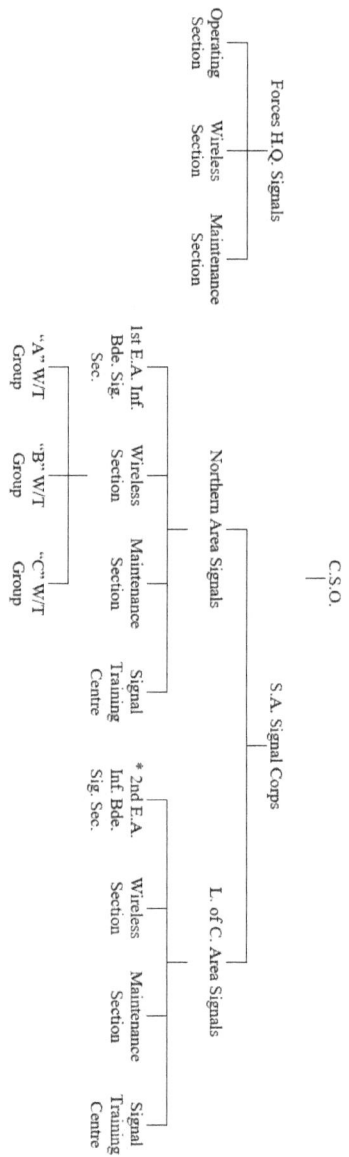

C.S.O.

- **Forces H.Q. Signals**
  - Operating Section
  - Wireless Section
  - Maintenance Section

- **S.A. Signal Corps**
  - **Northern Area Signals**
    - 1st E.A. Inf Bde. Sig. Sec.
      - "A" W/T Group
      - "B" W/T Group
      - "C" W/T Group
    - Wireless Section
    - Maintenance Section
    - Signal Training Centre
  - **L. of C. Area Signals**
    - * 2nd E.A. Inf. Bde. Sig. Sec.
    - Wireless Section
    - Maintenance Section
    - Signal Training Centre

* 2nd E.A. Brigade Signal Section now in Northern Area

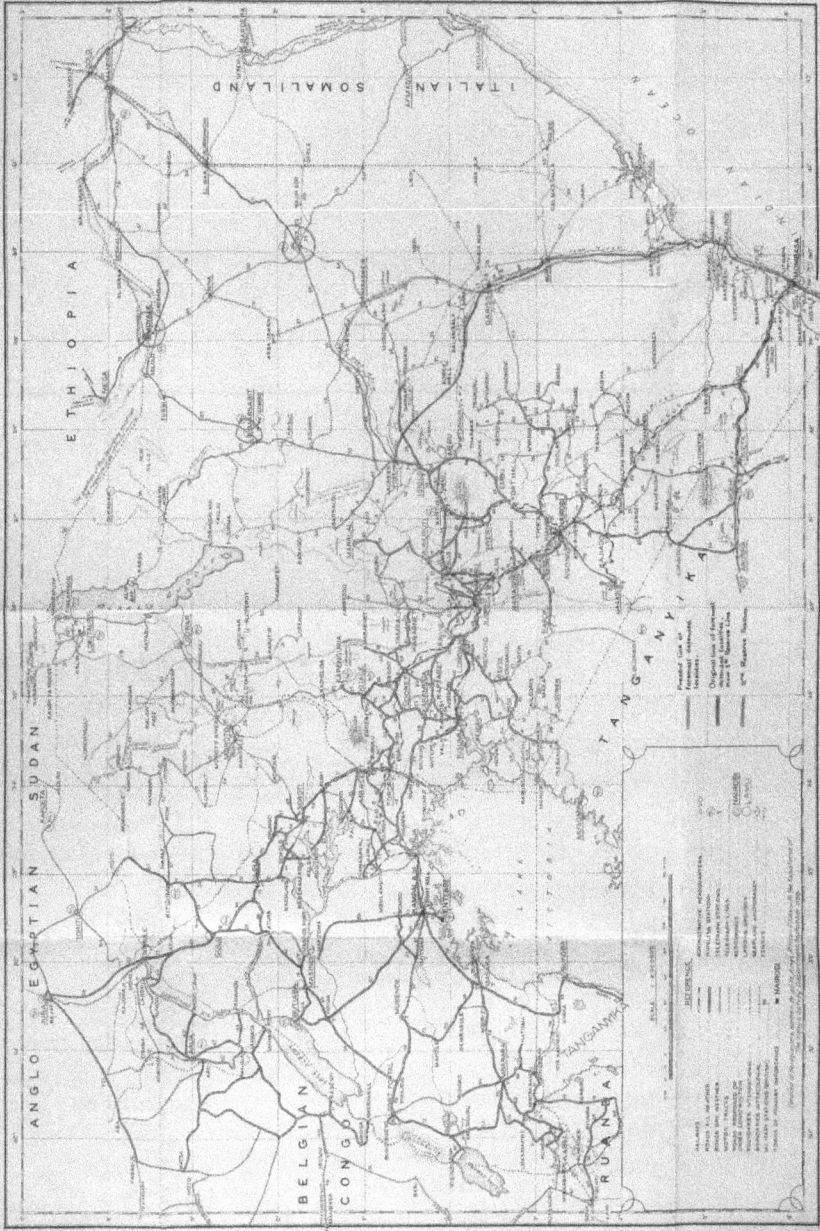

MILITARY COMMUNICATIONS MAP
KENYA AND UGANDA

See online larger version

FILE CREAF. 53
SECRET.

LOCATION STATEMENT.

<u>Force Headquarters.</u>	Nairobi
22nd Mountain Battery, R.A.	Mbagathi, Nairobi
1st E.A. Light Battery	Mbagathi, Nairobi
1st Field Survey Company, E.A.E.	
Headquarters and Map Production Section	Dar-es-Salaam
Field Topographical Section	Isiolo
2nd Field Topographical Section	Wajir
3rd Field Topographical Section	Nairobi - Details Camp
1st Field Company, E.A.E. less 2 sections	Malindi
1 Section	Malindi for Garissa
1 Water Section	Nanyuki
Mombasa Fortress.	
Coast Defence Battery, K.A.R.	Mombasa
Coast Defence Rifle Coy., K.A.R.	Mombasa
Force Headquarters Signals.	Kabete, Nairobi
Northern Area Signals	
Headquarters, Maintenance Section }	1st E.A. Inf. Bde.
Wireless Section, Signal School }	H.Q., Nairobi
Officers' School of Instruction	Nakuru
Depot Battalion, K.A.R., Kenya & Uganda.	Jinja
7th Battalion, K.A.R.	Bombo
A. Coy., 4th K.A.R.	Kamathia, Turkana
Uganda Police Service Company.	Lokitaung
Zanzibar Police.	Zanzibar
1st Battalion, E.A. Pioneers,	Garba Tulla
2nd Battalion, E.A. Pioneers (Less 2 Coys)	Isiola
1 Coy. 2nd En. E.A. Pioneers.	Wajir
1 Coy. 2nd En. E.A. Pioneers.	Nanyuki
E.A. Pack Donkey Corps.	Nairobi
<u>East African Army Service Corps.</u>	
Headquarters, E.A.A.S.C.	Nairobi
Main Supply Depot.	Nairobi
M.T. Training Centre and Depot	Nairobi
Vehicle Reception Depot.	Nairobi
Main M.T. Stores.	Nairobi

2.

<u>East Africa Army Service Corps. (Contd.)</u>

Heavy Repair Shop (nucleus) (under civil arrangements)	Nairobi
No. 1. M.T. Training School.	Bombo
No. 2. M.T. Training School less Detachment.	Zomba
No. 2. M.T. Training School Detachment.	Lusaka
No. 25 Battery Ammunition Coy.	Nairobi
A. Group Field Supply Depot.	Nanyuki
A. Group No. 1. Bus Coy.	Nanyuki
A. Group No. 14 Supply Coy.	Nanyuki
A. Group No. 6 Ammunition Coy.	Nanyuki
B. Group Headquarters, E.A.A.S.C.	Nanyuki
B. Group Field Supply Depot.	Nanyuki
B. Group No. 2. Bus Coy.	Nanyuki
B. Group No. 15 Supply Coy.	Nanyuki
B. Group No. 7 Ammunition Coy.	Nanyuki
C. Group Headquarters, E.A.A.S.C. (nucleus)	Kitale
C. Group No. 1. Sec. No. 20 Supply Coy.	Kitale
C. Group Field Supply Depot (nucleus).	Kitale
No. 17 Supply Coy. (Less 1 Sec)	Ngong, Nairobi
No. 17 Supply Coy 1 Section	Kitale
C. Group Field Supply Depot (Detachment)	Mariakani
C. Group 2 Sec. No. 20 Supply Coy.	Mariakani
C. Group 2 Sec. No. 5 Bus Coy.	Mariakani
C. Group 2 Sec. No. 5 Bus Coy.	Lokitaung
C. Group 1 Sec. No. 9 Ammunition Coy.	Mariakani
D. Group Headquarters, E.A.A.S.C.	Ngong, Nairobi
D. Group Field Supply Depot.	Ngong, Nairobi
D. Group H.Q. & 2 Sec. No.3. Bus Coy.	Ngong, Nairobi
D. Group H.Q. & 2 Sec. No.16. Supply Coy.	Ngong, Nairobi
D. Group H.Q. & 2 Sec. No. 8 Ammn. Coy.	Ngong, Nairobi
D. Group No. 24 Res. M.T. Coy. (Less 1 Sec.)	Ngong, Nairobi.

3

East Africa Army Service Corps (Contd.)

E. Group Headquarters E.A.A.S.C.	Ngong, Nairobi
No. 4 Bus Coy. (T.T.) (Less 1 Sec)	Ngong, Nairobi
No. 4 Bus Coy. (T.T.) 1 Sec.	Lokitaung
No. 10 Ammunition Coy.	Ngong, Nairobi
F. Group Headquarters } in process of	
2½ Res. M.T. Coys. } formation	Jinja
Supply Depot in process of formation	Jinja
Nyasaland Res. M.T. Coy.	due Ngong, Nairobi 17.12.39
Reserve M.T. Company	Zanzibar

Local British Forces.

1st Battalion, Kenya Regiment (T.A.)	Kampala
Kenya Defence Force Headquarters.	Nairobi

1st East Africa Infantry Brigade Headquarters

1st E. A. Brigade Signals.	Nairobi
2nd Battalion K.A.R.	
Headquarters & 3 Companies	Mbagathi, Nairobi
1 Company (D)	Arusha for Nairobi
3rd Battalion, K.A.R.	
Headquarters & 4 Companies	Jeans School, Nairobi
4th Battalion, K.A.R.	
Headquarters & 2 Companies	Malindi
1 Company (less 1 platoon)	Nairobi
1 Platoon	Garissa

2nd East Africa Infantry Brigade Headquarters

2nd E.A. Brigade Signals.	Nanyuki
1st Battalion, K.AR. (less 1 Coy.)	Isiolo
1 Company (D)	Wajir
5th Battalion, K.A.R.	
Headquarters & 3 Companies	Nanyuki
1 Company (C)	Moyale
6th Battalion, K.A.R. (less 1 Coy)	Nanyuki
1 Company (B)	Nakuru

Royal Air Force.

Headquarters.	Nairobi
Headquarters No. 1 Squadron S.R.A.F.	Nairobi
A. Flight S.R.A.F.	Nairobi
B. Flight S.R.A.F.	Nairobi

4

Royal Air Force (Contd.)
East Africa Auxiliary Air Unit
    No. 2 Flight (Training)   Nairobi
    No. 1 Flight (Inter-communication)   Nairobi
    No. 3 Flight Coastal Patrol.   Nairobi
    Air Defence Unit Coastal Patrol   Nairobi

East Africa Medical Corps.
Headquarters,   Nairobi
Uganda Field Ambulance Coy.   Jinja
Kenya Field Ambulance Company.   Athi River (For Mbagathi)
Tanganyika Field Ambulance Company. Isiolo
Zanzibar Field Ambulance Company.   Zanzibar
Uganda M.A.C.   Kabete, Nairobi
Kenya M.A.C.   Kabete, Nairobi
Tanganyika M.A.C.   Isiolo
Uganda C.C.S.   Kabete, Nairobi
Kenya C.C.S.   Kabete, Nairobi
Tanganyika C.C.S.   Nanyuki
2nd Field Ambulance   In course of formation
                                   at Dar-es-Salaam

East Africa Ordnance Corps.
Headquarters.   Nairobi
Ordnance Base Ammunition Depot.   Nairobi
Ordnance Base Depot.   Nairobi
Lines of Communication.
Headquarters – L. of C.   Dar-es-Salaam
L. of C. Area Signals.   Dar-es-Salaam
1st Northern Rhodesia Regiment
    Headquarters & 2 Companies   Moshi
    1 Company.   Arusha
    A. Company.   Iringa
2nd Northern Rhodesia Regiment.   Lusaka
2nd/6th Battalion K.A.R.   In course of formation
                                     at Moshi

Tanganyika Infantry Depot.   Dar-es-Salaam
Nyasaland Infantry Depot.   Zomba

5

Lines of Communication (Contd.)

Tanganyika Reserve

M.T. Coy.	2 Sections	Arusha
	2 Sections	Dar-es-Salaam
1. M.T. Company.		Blantyre
1. Heavy Repair Shop.		Blantyre
L. of C. Area Ordnance Base Depot.		Dar-es-Salaam
Ordnance Base Ammunition Depot.		Dar-es-Salaam

Distribution: -
Military Headquarters, Middle East.
Secretary, C.P.L.O.
G.S.O.1.
G.S.O.2. (I)
A.A.Q.M.G.
D.A.Q.M.G.
C.S.O.
D.A.A.G.
A.D.O.S.
O/C Best African Army Postal Service
Commandant Local British Forces and Nairobi Area.

File.

16th December, 1939.

[Sgd J. Moysey]

Major.
GENERAL STAFF.

AIR FORCES IN EAST AFRICA

Immediately prior to the outbreak of war,
No. 225 (Bomber) Squadron Royal Air Force, stationed in
Nairobi, moved to the Sudan. It was replaced shortly
afterwards by the arrival of No.1 Squadron Southern
Rhodesia Air Force,

The Royal Air Force Headquarters Staff remaining
in Nairobi after the departure of No. 235 (Bomber) Squadron
was inadequate to operate a detached force in the field
without any maintenance organisation behind it. Plans
that had previously been agreed upon between the Governor
of Kenya and the Air Officer Commanding-in-Chief Royal
Air Force Middle East were therefore put into effect,
whereby the resources of Wilson Airways Staff and such
civilian technical man power as was available in Kenya
were pooled to service and maintain the Southern Rhodesia
Air Force, and the essential mail services and air
communications required in war, All Civilian aircraft were
commandeered under an Ordinance signed by the Governor of
Kenya.

It was found possible to form and operate the
following Units: -

> No.1 Squadron Southern Rhodesia Air Force
> Communication Flight at Nairobi
> Training Flight at Nairobi
> Reconnaissance Flight at Mombasa
> Reconnaissance Flight at Dar-es-Salaam
> Communication Flight at Dar-es-Salaam.

No.1 Squadron Southern Rhodesia Air Force,
consists of five Audax and three Hart aircraft. The Unit
can operate as two separate and self contained detachments
in the field.

2.

The Communication Flights consist mostly of Wilson Airways aircraft with certain privately owned civilian aircraft added. Their duties are:-

     (i) Military communications and ferrying of Senior Government Officials and Serving officers.

     (ii) Local, and Central African Postal services.

     (iii) Special Postal or Communication flights as may be necessary.

The Reconnaissance Flights at Mombasa and Dar-es-Salaam

     (1) Maintain a close watch on all movements of shipping.

     (ii) Escort vessels arriving at or departing from Ports.

     (iii) Carry out certain specified patrols on the look-out for enemy warships and submarines.

APPENDIX "L"

"A" BRANCH DIFFICULTIES

1. "A" Branch Staff.

On the opening of Force Headquarters the then Staff Officer Local Forces was appointed D.A.A.G.

In addition to starting the "A" office he had to hand over his pre-war duties to another officer, a task which took more than a week. He had no staff experience.

The Staff Captain "A" was a temporary officer during the great war, who had served with K.A.R. but who also had no previous staff experience.

He was first warned for duty on 28th August.

No clerks trained or otherwise were available. Two female typists were engaged.

2. Manuals & Army Forms.

No provision had been made for these and none were available. A Manual of Military Law was borrowed from Northern Brigade. This Manual is now shared between Force Headquarters, 1st E.A. Infantry Brigade and the Attorney General of Kenya.

A copy of King's Regulations unamended, but with amendments attached, arrived from home at the end of November.

No Army Orders or Army Council Instructions have yet been received.

Fortunately Colonel Bishop brought from home with him a monthly Army List April 1959 and a Quarterly Army List April 1939.

A half-yearly Army List dated December 1938, was borrowed from a Nairobi Club.

... 2

2.

3. Provision of Officer Reinforcements.

Pre war policy in Kenya seems to have been to ignore and systematically discourage R.A.R.O.'s and retired temporary officers with war experience. No arrangements had been made to classify these or to ear-mark them for employment. Practically none held mobilization orders in peace time.

Officer reinforcements for the A.S.C. were selected by local man power committees, often without much consideration.

Officer reinforcements were to come almost entirely from the ranks of the Kenya Regiment, which had been in existence for 18 months, and had done two ten day camps.

Somewhat precipitately these were selected, authorised to wear uniform of officers, and posted to K.A.R. Battalions by Northern Brigade before Force Headquarters assumed control.

These appointments could not be confirmed. Not only was very considerable heart burning caused to those concerned, but a very dangerous disciplinary situation had been created. In effect, a class of uncommissioned officer had been created which derived its authority from nowhere.

4. Provision of British Other Ranks reinforcements.

The pre war policy in this matter was the same as for the officers, though the consequences were not so serious. Still, a lot of good material, consisting of ex-N.C.O.'s and men with war experience, was ignored.

5. Commissions.

The question of the granting of commissions had hardly been considered, and in Kenya not at all. In other Territories the Governors ruled that they could grant

commissions/

3.

commissions in the K.A.R., R.O. and apply subsequently for the Secretary of State's authority. The Governor of Kenya ruled otherwise, and a complete deadlock was reached, The main difficulty which presented itself was the fact that Imperial Emergency Commissions would only carry Imperial Rates of Pay, and it was realised that it would be necessary for all officers to hold some sort of local commission.

To date some 600 gentlemen have received commissions (most of them 2 commissions) and numerous acting promotions have been made.

In the absence of an Assistant Military Secretary at Force Headquarters, this has been a whole time task for the Staff Captain "A".

6. Establishments.

With the exception of the E.A.A.S.C. no establishments for any administrative units existed. These all had to be worked out.

In the absence of a Staff Duties Branch at Force Headquarters, this work was at first undertaken by "A", but when the military situation permitted, it was transferred to "G".

7. Legal.

Authority for the appointment of a D.J.A.G. has just been received,

The legal position has from time to time caused great anxiety. Not only does "A" Branch require a knowledge of the Army Act, but also of five different Ordinances in Kenya alone, governing the Defence Forces of that Colony.

These Ordinances are so worded that a part only of the Army Act is made applicable to the forces raised under them.

.... 4

4.

In November, when the formation of the new units, including the E.A.A.S.C., was well under way, the Law Officers of Kenya ruled that my action in raising them was illegal, and that in consequence the men of these units were not subject to military law.

Yet another Military Ordinance was therefore passed through Legislative Council to legalize the position.

The lack of a trained legal adviser has been much felt during the past three months.

ORDNANCE SERVICES

1. My Assistant Director of Ordnance Services did not arrive here till the 8th September to find no organisation whatever for the Ordnance Services nor any trained personnel with which to start it. The position here at that time was one of each commanding Officer doing his best for his own Unit under very difficult circumstances with absolutely no organisation or control of expenditure [sic] Owing to the lack of any trained personnel the Assistant Director of Ordnance Services had not only to function in the capacity as head of the service but also had to train what inexperienced personnel he could find, establish his Depots and maintain his ledgers and accounts[.] The position as regards personnel is only now beginning to adjust itself and should my Force be ordered overseas the shortage of trained personnel would cripple my Ordnance Services. It is well nigh impossible for the Head of a Service to compete with the requirements of an expanding force, foresee and cater for increasing demands by indent or purchase, and at the same time organise and train personnel to administer the Service for which he is responsible.

2. Situation of Ordnance Services

On the outbreak of war the Ordnance stocks in East Africa were, to all intents and purposes, nil. The Force has increased from roughly four thousand to approximately twenty thousand and the requirements for such expansion can well be appreciated. There was no reserve of uniform, clothing, equipment or boots. As regards these articles it was possible to resort to local purchase and in this respect the local Tender Board has

been most helpful in acquiring all that was available.
and saving unnecessary expenditure. As regards
clothing and equipment it has also been possible to
procure and manufacture in the country bush-shirts,
shorts, boots, blankets, and leather equipment. My
requirements of socks, puttees, British Warms and web
equipment, cannot be met and the shortage at the
moment is really serious. Neither have I received
any compasses, binoculars, web equipment, respirators
or anti-gas stores from England

3. Arms and Ammunition
    The arms and ammunition situation in Kenya
was still less satisfactory and can be tabulated as
follows:-

Infantry Weapons	Position as at outbreak of war	Position as at 31.12.1939
Guns Bren,	44	131
Anti-tank Rifles,	24	46
Mortars M.L.3",	2	3
Lewis Guns	130	226
Vickers Guns	43	79
Ammunition		
.306 Mk. VII	2,332,528	14,485,154
Tracer	7,397	16,770
Anti-tank	1,950	3,290
Bombs 3" H.E.	780	6,153

4. TENTAGE
    An almost complete lack of tentage has
caused me much anxiety in connection with the housing of
the greatly increased numbers. This dearth of tentage
would have made it almost impossible for the Medical
Units to have worked on a mobile basis should war have
come in September. A limited amount of used tentage

3

has been acquired by local purchase and a further supply is shortly expected from India. I must stress. however, the danger of expecting a force, operating in a country like this, to find itself with a complete lack of tentage.

5. R.E. STORES

No supply of R.E. Stores such as barbed wire, pickets, sand-bags etc., existed in the country. Sand-bags have now been produced in Kenya and over the last two months the necessary supplies of barbed wire and pickets have been made good.

6. ORDNANCE DEPOTS.

Owing to climatic conditions, being centrally located, and connected by rail with the port of Mombasa, Nairobi was chosen as the main Ordnance centre. A suitable building, containing offices and a good store of about thirty thousand square feet, with overhead gantries and rail siding, was rented and has proved eminently suitable as an Ordnance Depot. My main ammunition depot has also been located at Nairobi[.] In view of possible hostilities with Italy I have chosen Nanyuki as a railhead and I have located there small Ordnance and ammunition depots holding approximately a third of my stocks.

7. WORKSHOPS,

The Kenya Uganda Railways & Harbours have been most helpful in placing their well equipped workshops in Nairobi at my disposal. The workmanship is excellent. and they have already produced a trial mortar which is in no way inferior to the Home product. Forty eight more

4

have now been approved and are in course of manufacture
The South African Government have offered a supply of
sights, which cannot be made locally, but approval to
accept this offer is still awaited from the War
Office.

EAST AFRICA COMMAND.

PAY, SERVICES AND FINANCIAL CONTROL.

My Command Paymaster arrived in Kenya on 1st September, 1939.

The first major problem to be faced was the fixing of rates of pay for Officers.. This was a very complicated matter, as Officers of all classes and grades were called up or reported for duty. Although, with a view to having a common scale to all, I recommended that every Officer (other than the few Imperial Officers at Headquarters) should be paid at African Colonial Forces scales of pay, the War Office by their telegram 57818 of 24th September, 1939, placed the Regular Army Reserve of Officers (approximately 100) on British rates of pay and allowances. This raised obvious difficulties, first as regards the inequality of these rates compared with locally commissioned Officers serving in the same Unit, and secondly, control and administration of their pay and allowances, etc., from Force Headquarters. Local Paymasters had not the necessary British Regulations to issue the pay and allowances, and if issued by the Command Paymaster, the difficulties in obtaining particulars of their Service, status for married rates of allowances etc., were almost insurmountable, in the vast Area covered by this Command with very poor communications. These facts were represented to both the Colonial and War Offices in numerous telegrams ranging over a period from 9.9.39, until, finally on 21.10.39, the War Office agreed to all R.A.R.O. being placed on same footing for pay as those of African Colonial Forces, subject to stoppage of retired pay where drawn. Throughout this period also, necessitating

constant/--

2.

/constant cables, representations were submitted to U.K.
regarding Command pay for certain heads of Departments at
H.Q., civilian employees and various Military appointments
under the Colonial Office before the War.

One of the biggest difficulties in connection
with the issue of pay to Officers is due to the fact that
the new rates, drawn up in peace time and brought into
force on 15th September, 1939, quote a qualifying service
element for each rank, i.e. 3 years for a Lieutenant, 8
years for a Captain, etc. The question of fixing a rate
of pay for Officers who have been appointed Acting
Lieutenants, Captains and Majors to fill establishment
and who have no qualifying service element (applicable
to the majority of Officers called up here) was referred
to the Secretary of State for the Colonies, but no decision
has yet been received.

The difficulties experienced by paymasters
in endeavouring to arrive at some basis on which to pay
these Officers, and the extra work involved in making
subsequent adjustments working with native staffs will be
appreciated. A further difficulty affecting the issue of
pay is due to the decision to give Officers and N.C.O.'s of
the African Colonial Forces serving on the 14th September
the option of electing to draw either existing or new scales
of pay. To date, after 3 months lapse of time, these options
are still in process of being exercised, due to various
considerations which have been submitted by those concerned,
and wherein protracted correspondence has ensued. In
Particular the position of Reserve Officers of the King's
African Rifles called up before 14th September, 1939, as
regards right of election to the old rates of pay is still
not cleared up.

Another/

3.

Another question which has required consideration is that affecting rates of pay to be fixed for civilian personnel, (typists, stenographers, clerks etc.,) together with scales of pay for African personnel of newly raised units. In these cases, consultation and agreement with the five territories has resulted in an infinity of discussion and correspondence owing to varying local conditions, in an effort to co-ordinate the standard of remuneration over the whole Command.

Further complicated issues occurred in respect of troops belonging to Southern Rhodesia moved to fill War Establishments in other territories. These personnel are on a lower scale of pay than African Colonial Forces.

COMMON CHARGES ACCOUNT.

On 2nd October, 1939, a telegram was received from the War Office setting out certain principles for guidance in relation to the incidence of charge arising in maintaining the Forces in East Africa.

This question is one that has raised a great amount of correspondence and diversity of opinion as to liability with the Territories concerned. In the estimates submitted to the War Office on 4th November, 1939, it was pointed out that disagreement as to allocation of expenditure (apart from pay and allowances of troops) was inevitable when final analysis is called for. Moreover, it was apparent that I had no control whatever over what items were being placed in the Common Charges account in the various Territories.

This procedure, in the considered opinion of financial authorities, appeared to be almost unworkable in its existing form, and suggestions for an alternative scheme/---

4.

/scheme, based on acceptance of all charges by the War Office, with annual contributions from the Colonies to a sum provided for in 1939 Military estimates plus 25% were submitted by the Conference of East Africa Governors.

Representations covering these considerations were submitted to the War Office on 11.10.39. This resulted in the formation of an East Africa Pay Corps to run the Common Charges Account, and administer all pay and allowances of Military personnel in East Africa receiving pay from Colonial source. (W.O. Telegram 59295 of 19.10.39.)

Constitution of a Military Audit Staff, to audit all Military expenditure was also submitted to War Office and approved 26.11.39.

Financial control and accounting will be simplified when I assure complete financial responsibility on behalf of the War Office on 1st January, 1940, War Office Telegram 61850 dated 9.12.39, refers,

FINANCIAL CONTROL.

It will give some idea of the scope of the responsibilities of my Command Paymaster, who combines with his pay duties that of Financial Adviser, when it is realised that the East African Command covers an area of over 1,000,000 square miles.

In this dual capacity he has had to act alone, no other Officer of his Corps being provided for in War Establishment. With but three other ranks to assist him (two of whom have had very limited command experience) the Staff provided has been quite inadequate to enable him to devote the proper time to the major questions of financial control, administration and policy.

From the inception of this Command a very large/---

5

/large works services programme covering road construction,
temporary barracks, bridging, etc., had to be undertaken,
spread over five territories wherein the necessity for
centralized financial control was paramount, particularly
as it was found that Local Commanders had their own somewhat
grandiose ideas as to their requirements and had acted in
the earlier stages entirely on their own responsibility.
This state of affairs has required strong measures to curb:
as a case in point the equipment of a mess for eleven women
motor drivers at Dar es Salaam, based on these standards,
cost over £250 and appropriate action has been taken.

Road estimates and barrack accommodation
which in the first few weeks were undertaken by the P.W.D.,
were also planned on such lavish scales as to constitute
a very definite infringement of all the safeguards affecting
economy and waste. The urgent requirements of importunate
Local Commanders in regard to messing, accommodation and
equipment, road construction, housing, subsistence etc.,
were also found, on analysis, in very many cases to be
capable of adjustment on much more economical lines, in the
very definite consideration that capital expenditure for any
service in this country will bring small return in terms of
money, when W.D. property comes into a very limited market
for realization after the War.

Perhaps the most disturbing feature in the
purchase of Stores, transport etc., is that vehicles and
petrol in particular were requisitioned by the civil
authorities during the mobilization period. In the case
of lorries no less than 1,200 were requisitioned in which
practically all were without tools or equipment, necessitating
a sum approximating £66,000 to be spent on making them fit
for the road, whilst numbers will need to be condemned as
altogether/---

6.

/altogether unserviceable,

About one and a quarter million gallons of petrol were also taken over by local Government, and as a necessary precaution were stored all over the country (in tins). Leakage and evaporation is taking place both in storage and transit. These questions of requisitioning of transport and storage of petrol will require earnest consideration and action with territories concerned regarding onus of responsibility. I have referred to both of them in more detail in Appendix B Supply and Transport.

No Army stationery forms have been received from the United Kingdom, The limited number of Regulations available are those brought out by certain Officers in the hurried emergency conditions of their departure from England. and have had to be borrowed by various services, in most cases from the Command Pay Office.

Certain Officers pay sheets are also not yet available and a cabled request has been despatched to the War Office.

Attached hereto is a copy of a letter on the financial aspect of the situation which was sent to the Under Secretary of State, the War Office, LONDON.

EAST AFRICA FORCE HEADQUARTERS,
NAIROBI. KENYA.
25th December, 1989.

The Under Secretary of State,
The War Office,
LONDON. S.W.1.

I have to acknowledge receipt of your letter F.I.B.M. 988 of the 8th December, 1939, regarding the question of financial commitments in this Command.

I welcome these observations, as it gives me an opportunity to present to you some kind of picture – a complete one would scarcely be possible of the financial difficulties and complex situations inherent in the building up of a new Command, wherein I have been called upon to exercise control of expenditure over a Command embracing the dependencies of Kenya, Uganda, Tanganyika, Nyasaland, Northern Rhodesia and Zanzibar assisted by staff of three clerks, These clerks form my pay staff, two of whom have had very limited Command experience.

You refer to the fact that conditions in East Africa are not entirely favourable to the normal routine of administration, and that many questions cannot be anticipated owing to the absence of a trained peace time Staff. It will perhaps also be appreciated that this Command covers an area of approximately one million square miles, with very poor communications, and ever. by working to all hours of the night, it has not been possible at times, to compass everything into the twenty four hours of the day.

Many and very large commitments were entered into by the civil authorities on behalf of the War Department at the time of mobilization and before Headquarters was in a position to take control. These include requisitioning and purchase of motor transport, purchase and storage of one and à quarter million gallons of petrol, all over the country, works services, etc., etc., involving in my opinion, in many cases, an unwarranted waste of public money and material, In this connection, in particular, I have been called upon to make very strong representations, which will subsequently be referred to by the General Officer Commanding in a separate despatch.

These are perhaps major considerations but they form only a small part of the complex problems here, wherein apart from financial questions, I have been called upon for advice from every branch of the Service. It is to be observed also that a very large number of these matters has to be referred to the political side and the coordination of interests and financial obligations of all the dependencies has at times been extremely vexatious. As a case in point, I might mention the fixing of rates of pay for civilian employees, where the objections of every Government regarding wages as affected by local conditions, cannot be lightly regarded, and the subsequent adoption of uniform scales, has necessitated long and tedious correspondence. The working. and incidence of charge regarding the Common Charges Account
too,/

Cont'd..........

2.

/too, has presented many difficulties up to date. In the prolonged correspondence affecting the Status of the Regular Army Reserve of Officers, the commissioning of officers to local forces, the adoption of new scales of pay for African Colonial Forces, the formation of the East African Pay Corps and Audit Staff, etc., I have had to take a very active part in the absence of anyone qualified so to act, and though it is appreciated that they were questions requiring mature consideration by the Home Authorities, the belated replies which were inevitable, rendered the whole aspect of pay questions more difficult and complicated day by day.

Local commanders too, thousands of miles away, incurred expenditure for works services, stores, stationery, equipment of messes, etc., far beyond their powers, until the centralization of control of expenditure in Headquarters authority was finally accomplished. The building of accommodation, bridges, roads, etc., and the necessity for same, over such a vast area, with poor communications and lack of a proper submission or mental picture of requirements, has required my vigilant attention, but acting entirely alone, both as Command Paymaster and Financial Adviser, I am bound to say, there have been times, when I have found it difficult in the extreme in securing the proper and effective control, consistent with the regulated procedure at Home, The situation in general with new staffs etc. at the various headquarters has been so fluid, that the insistence on certain principles, as provided by regulations, in many cases has not been possible, and in many cases a realization of local difficulties, governed by common sense, has at times been a determining factor. Belated receipt of instructions, regulations affecting other services, officers pay sheets, Army orders and A.C.T. has also contributed to this consideration.

It is no doubt the fact, that in the wide range of all the questions referred to, there is an ultimate financial reaction, and it was inevitable that in the urgency of many of these matters, reference to the Financial Adviser was completely overlooked by the Staff Officers concerned. It will be realized that there are few Regular Officers in this country and the General Officer Commanding has been forced to utilize all these to train Units, with the exception. of those appointed from Home to Headquarters, totalling seven (including Heads of Services).

Force Headquarters has therefore been primarily constituted by appointing officers with previous Great War experience, who are too old to take their places in the field and are without any staff experience. However, in my day to day insistence on this necessity, procedure in this respect has become more stabilized,

In this connection, I have kept a copy of all my observations raised on the hundred and one issues involved, which I shall produce at the appropriate time. In their submission, I hope to convey some broad idea of the formidable task presented, in establishing financial control on a proper basis in this country.

These observations are no doubt somewhat irrelevant to the points raised in your memorandum, but I feel bound to put these facts before you and a copy has been placed before the General Officer Commanding, and my own branch at the War Office.

Cont'd....

3.

I should like to emphasize very strongly that the General Officer Commanding has supported me in every particular, regarding the spending of public money in this Command. His policy throughout has been an insistence on financial stringency consistent with requirements in relation to urgent military necessity.

(Signed) A. S. S. Herbert.
Bt. Colonel.
Command Paymaster & Financial Adviser,
East Africa Force.

Copy to War Office (F. q.)

P.S. As regards communications, I might also have
mentioned that the Air Mail Service runs once a week only
in this country and even in these circumstances, it takes
a week or ten days to receive a reply.

(Signed)　A.S.S.H.

MEDICAL SITUATION
EAST AFRICA: SEPTEMBER DECEMBER
1939

Prior to the outbreak of hostilities arrangements had been made for the formation of certain Medical Units in the East African Territories. When war was declared, these units were mobilized. The calling up of Government Medical Officers, Sanitary Inspectors and trained African personnel disorganized the civil Medical administration in the Territories concerned, and although this was not very apparent in the initial stages, it had a very definite re-action at a later date when the threat of immediate active hostilities became less threatening.

Many difficulties were encountered, and it is proposed to deal with them under their appropriate headings.

EAST AFRICAN MEDICAL CORPS

Although medical units were organized and mobilized, there was no legal authority for their existence. Medical Officers wore uniform and held ranks to which they were not legally entitled. They trained their men on military lines, although they were not in a position to note out any form of punishment for military offences.

The East African Dependencies Military Units Ordinance 1959 was passed in early December. This Ordinance legalised for the first time the position of the East African Medical Corps but has, in doing so, introduced many complications. The previous attestations are now void, and all men have to be attested afresh. If, as seems

probable,

2.

probable, a number of men refuse to accept the new terms of service, the medical units will have to begin training afresh, and their three months of intensive training will have been wasted.

MEDICAL SUPPLIES,

Prior to the outbreak of war the governments of Uganda, Kenya and Tanganyika each allotted the sum of £15,000 for the purchase of a reserve of essential drugs and dressings. The use to which this reserve was to be put seems to have been interpreted differently by the Governments concerned,

Medical units were to be formed and equipped on a definite scale, and it must be admitted that, in most cases, this was carried out, but a large number of the vehicles, evidently hurriedly assembled, were totally unfit for service, and had to be overhauled and reconditioned on arrival in Kenya.

Had it not been for the good services of the Kenya Civil Medical Department it would have been utterly impossible for medical units and Medical Officers responsible for the treatment of sick and injured to carry out their duties.

When the situation was appreciated a Base Depot of Medical Stores was asked for from England, but the first consignment of these stores cannot arrive before January 1940. The prospect was not very bright until the Kenya Government came to our aid and offered a bulk issue of supplies tide us over this difficult period.

A suitable building has been requisitioned and taken over for use as a Base Depot Store for the supplies ordered from home.

3/

3

PERSONNEL FOR MEDICAL UNITS.

As stated previously, medical units were staffed
from Civil Government sources, which caused some disorganization
of the Civil Medical administration.

As time went on the effects of this began to take
effect, and requests began to be received to release officers,
Sanitary Inspectors, and trained African personnel. These were
met as far as possible on condition that their services would
be available in an emergency.

However, as time went on and the prospect of
immediate local hostilities lessened, the demands for the
return of personnel increased until a point has been reached
where, if the demands are met in full, or without replacement,
it would be impossible to maintain the military Medical
Services in anything like a reasonable state of preparedness
or efficiency.

HOSPITALS.

Generally speaking the Civil Hospitals in Kenya
only suffice th [sic] cater for the Civil population. It has therefore bee necessary to open Military hospitals for Europeans
and Africans at Nairobi and Nanyuki, where are the larger
concentrations of troops.